Mirror Appointment Setting:

How to Build Long-Term B2B Prospect Relationships Step-by Step

By Aren Benoit

First Edition

Published by:
Eliyora Entertainment, LLC
477 Peace Portal Drive, Suite 107-420,
Blaine, WA 98230

Written as Aren Benoit by Sherese Chrétien for
Eliyora Entertainment, LLC
All personas and concepts created by Sherese Chrétien

Cover image by: Lucidio Studio, Inc.
Cover design by: Brad Joyce

Printed by CreateSpace, in the USA

ISBN-13: 978-1492117865
ISBN-10: 1492117862
Available from Amazon.com, CreateSpace.com, and other retail outlets
Also available on Kindle and other devices

To my family. Thank you for patiently listening.

Contents

Preface

If Star Wars can do it, so can I! This book is the first I am writing in a series I will be doing on what I refer to as Mirror Business, because Mirror Appointment Setting is currently on my plate. We'll work our way backwards – and forwards from here to complete a series of books encompassing a philosophy that I have shared with many clients in many industries and honed over 30-plus successful years as a business development specialist. I hope you will find this book, and the rest of the Mirror Business series, vital to building sustainable practices & long-term business relationships.

A Note on Format

I've decided to format my books the way I've always wished others would format their books for me. I love it when gadgets and gizmos come with a Quick Start Guide AND a Reference Manual. I'm always going to try to get by with the Quick Start Guide, and then, if I get stuck, I'll have to take the time to dig into the Manual. I assume others are like me, and wish "How To" books – no matter the topic – would do the same thing! So I'm going to do it! For all of you kindred spirits out there who'd rather be doing rather than reading, here is your Quick Start Guide.

Following the Quick Start Guide, you will find a "Why" section, if you are so inclined to dig into the gears of my business philosophy, then a "How" Manual section, going into step-by-step detail, and last, a bibliography you can use to deepen your understanding. My goal is to write "zero fluff" books as a courtesy to my valued readers – I'm hoping this format strategy will help me succeed in achieving that goal.

This particular book is speaking directly to those of you who are tasked with setting business-to-business appointments for a salesperson or sales team. Sales Managers, I advise you to read the "Quick Start Guide" and up to **Part III: Mirror Marketing Training** to set up your system and inform your hiring process, then hire your Mirror Appointment Setters and hand them this book as their training manual to do the rest.

Introduction

Every sales team dreams of filling all of their appointments. And isn't it fun to project sales for all of those potential appointments and dream "What if?!" But then reality sinks in. How do you get those appointments filled with qualified prospects? The never-ending challenge of sales is how to get in the door.

You could outsource to a call center with a cold call/blitzing approach – but let's face it – how do you like being on the receiving end of those blitzing calls? Once you've looked in the Mirror and admitted you don't like it, then imagine how your potential clients will feel – is that really the first impression you want to make on the clients with whom you hope to build long-lasting, mutually beneficial relationship? We all know the answer to that question.

We hope call centers will read this book and switch to my Mirror approach – wouldn't that be great?! Then you could outsource to them!

Until then, I'd like to suggest another option – creating your own appointment setting program tailored to your business and your prospective clients. I call it Mirror Appointment Setting. Over 30-plus years as a successful business development specialist, a mirror has become my metaphor for the most basic ethical foundation of any successful relationship – business or otherwise: The Golden Rule – treat others the way you wish to be treated, combined with a brutally honest, self-reflective accountability.

Yeah, I know, big, new revelation, huh?! Well, we all say it throughout our lives, and we all believe in it – but actually putting it into practice is a whole different story. I'm not here to promise you a magic appointment pill, I am here to promise you a step-by-step, sustainable appointment setting technique that has consistently catapulted my results, and the results of my clients, to short-term and long-term levels significantly higher than standard appointment setting approaches. It works! And it works more often and more consistently than any other approach – and I've tried them all over the years! That's why you're here, right? You want something that WORKS!

You do have to leave the "blitzing" mind-set behind, though. And there is absolutely no place in my business approach for a "dog-eat-dog" perspective. This technique is for those organizations striving to create and sustain a highly successful business over the long-haul, standing on a foundation of thoughtfully-constructed, reflective business relationships.

Let's begin.

Quick Start Guide

Items required:
- ➤ Comfortable, quiet space
- ➤ Computer(s)
- ➤ CRM Software with database sorting & scheduling capabilities
- ➤ Scrubbed, qualified Lead List in digital format
- ➤ Land-line Phone(s)
- ➤ Professional-Quality-Sound Headset(s)
- ➤ Toll Free Number
- ➤ Customized Scripts
- ➤ Qualifying Script (gathering Intel from gatekeepers only to qualify leads)
- ➤ DM Appointment Setting Script (Speaking to the Decision Maker)
- ➤ Marketing Email(s)
- ➤ Email Software

Step-by-Step Set-Up:
- ➤ CRM Database:
  - • Load Lead List into CRM Software
  - • Set CRM preferences to automatically roll scheduled calls & to-dos forward
  - • Enter the following Status IDs:
    - o Dead = OOB (out of business)
    - o DNC = do not call
    - o Disconnected = NIS (not in service) phone is disconnected

- o DM = Decision Maker Identified
- o Duplicate = duplicate lead
- o Existing Client = existing client identified
- o HOLD = DM hung up; DM will call if interested; seasonal; needs intel; networked leads
- o Lead = unreached lead
- o Not Qualified = NQ lead is not qualified
- o Out of Area = OOA decisions are made outside your market area
- o Past Appointment = held appointments
- o Phone Appointment = phone appointments referred to sales team
- o Prospect = Decision Maker reached and follow-up scheduled
- o Renewal = any renewal date or annual product/service review period identified
- o Scheduled Call Back (Month) = contact other than decision maker requested call back
- o Wrong Number = phone number reassigned

Getting Started – Step-by-Step

The goal of Mirror Appointment Setting is not only to set appointments with currently receptive prospects, but to create long-term prospect relationships with the vast majority of your leads, obtaining permission to continue to follow-up until they too are ready to move from prospect to appointment. How do you do this? Fundamentally, everything you say and do in regards to your prospects needs to be in line with what you would want said or done if you were them, with a long-term relationship in mind!

➤ Begin calling leads using your Qualifying Script to gather intel from receptionists.

➤ Set Status IDs as you gather intel.

➤ As you move qualified leads up the Status ID chain from DM to Prospect, begin sorting by Status ID to make your calling more efficient – for instance, only do Lead qualifying calls when DMs are not available, say early morning, during lunch or late afternoons.

➤ Once you have a significant set of DM Status IDs, layer an email marketing campaign in with your calling efforts, sending no more emails then you would like to receive if you were them (quarterly, bi-annually, annually are usually considered reasonable).

➤ Once you have streamlined your calling schedule, you should be able to perform 12-15 dials per hour among Status IDs DMs-Renewals-Prospects and an average of 20 dials per hour among Lead Status IDs.

➤ When DMs agree to a call back they become Prospects -- schedule a call back and follow through, as you literally, layer by layer, call back by call back, day-by-day, and year-by-year, "earn" the right to set an appointment with them.

➤ Getting permission to follow-up with them equals success, burning that bridge by impatience equals failure.

➤ When a Prospect agrees to set an appointment, verify and gather the necessary details, email an appointment confirmation, then confirm two days prior to the appointment. Great Job!

➤ Polite Persistence and Courteous Call Backs win the day.

➤ Create a "Follow-Up Service" Alliance with your Prospects and win the race long after all the blitzers fade away.

~~**~~

Mirror Appointment Setting

If you'd like more than the Quick Start Guide to get your Mirror Appointment Setting program set-up -- here we go. I'll first lay down the foundation of my approach -- the Why. Then, I'll take you through the step-by-step details -- the How. You'll be on your way to a new level of success in no time!

The Why of Mirror Appointment Setting

The Mirror as a Business Metaphor

There are many useful metaphoric layers of meaning for me within the idea of a Mirror, when it comes to business strategy – and even life strategy. Those of us who have been to lots and lots of sales training over the years might recall the concept of "mirroring," – or reflecting back our prospects' body language, and tone, in an effort to build empathetic rapport (Charny,1966; Kendon,1970; LaFrance, 1979, 1985; Scheflen, 1964) .

While somewhat useful, I always felt like that was just a surface technique and sort of fake (for me, anyway), and the real value I took from this tip-of-the-iceberg idea was to take it to a much deeper and more genuine level by simply reflecting on the Golden Rule and my own accountability. Not only should I be trying to "seem" like I'm empathizing, but how about actually empathizing. How about trying to imagine and be acutely aware of how it would feel to be in my prospect's shoes in any given moment, as I'm trying to persuade and convince them to see things my way – which is the case in any relationship, not just business. How about being constantly vigilant of my responsibilities in this mutually beneficial relationship I'm trying to create.

The results? Taking the extra time to go deeper always – and I do mean always – meant more success in whatever facet of business, or life in general, to which I applied what I came to call my "Mirror" strategy. You can call me very lazy – or very efficient. Either way, creating a long-lasting bridge, a long-term relationship, was always preferable and the Mirror technique is always how I was able to achieve that goal.

We all know what it takes to create a client (or any type of relationship for that matter) and that it takes a lot less to keep one. So am I lazy, wanting to invest the time and maximize each opportunity I encounter, using my Mirror approach, so I don't have to keep finding and burning through a bunch of opportunities over and over – or am I smart? You decide.

So the Mirror symbolizes not only the reflection of your prospect but also the reflection of yourself. It is an entire business (and life) philosophy, addressing all of the angles – your approach to business ethics, your approach to product/service production, your approach to marketing, your approach to profit, and your approach to being a corporate community citizen. It extends vertically from every macro to micro level of your business, and horizontally A-Z to every relationship of your business.

As I mentioned in the preface to this book, I will be compiling my Mirror Business Strategies series to provide you with the theory and application in detail. For now, we are drilling down our focus to applying my Mirror strategy to business-to-business appointment setting.

The Mirror Applied to Business-to-Business Appointment Setting

The phone has always been and continues to be an "edge tool" for me. It is the next best thing to being there, belly to belly, with your prospective client -- if done right. In nearly every sales situation I've ever faced or trained in across a wide landscape of industries, knowing how to "work" the phone edged my success and my clients' success past the nearest competitor, and in most cases by a significant "how did you do that!" margin.

We all have a negative view of using the phone for marketing because, well, we've all been victims! It has a negative perception only because, in most scenarios, it IS a negative experience -- even traumatic for both the caller and the called. If you ask the vast majority of salespeople who are expected to cold call what they like least about their job, they would say cold calling. If you ask businesses what they like least about salespeople who cold call them, they would say being cold called. So, there you have it!

Then why am I suggesting that you continue to use the phone as an edge tool in marketing, and why do I continue to use the phone with great success? Because applying my Mirror Strategy turns your phone from a cold calling monster into a "service call" ally – a marketing process opportunity to provide your prospects "high touch" until they become your clients.

Think again about what I told you Mirror means and apply that to using the phone as a marketing tool. Let's deconstruct the standard cold-calling and blitzing scenarios. When we're expected to do cold- calling, we're interrupting a Decision Maker to ask the time – well, not really, but we might as well be, because the Decision Maker and their company are a complete unknown to us that's why it's called "cold" calling.

We're asking a complete stranger to do business with us, even though we weren't polite enough to properly introduce ourselves (we're just an interrupting voice on the phone), or dedicated enough to gain proper knowledge of them or their business before asking them to take time away from their busy day to listen to us.

In most cases, when we're expected to do cold calling we are also blitzing, meaning we have no intention of calling businesses back or following up – our intent is to dial, dial, dial to find the "one-hit-wonders," the "low-hanging fruit."

We're not usually taking notes, (Why? If the business is not willing to set an immediate appointment, we're moving on!) or taking the time to fulfill the business' reasonable request to receive an introductory email – that would take too much time away from dial, dial, dial! We could even call it being a "phone player" – because we have one goal in mind, and we are not stopping our hunt to invest any time in creating a relationship. Dial, dial, dial!

With this approach, it is true we are probably able to do 40 dials an hour – but we have to stop and ask, at what expense? What have we left on the table? When you consider the "collateral damage" left in our wake – the slew of alienated businesses who definitely do remember the name of the instigating company and if the blitzing-cold-calling company ever did call them back they would get an ear full or just a quick, loud click! Is it worth it?

Do you really have an unlimited supply of prospective clients in your market area? How many bridges are you burning to get that small handful of one-hit-wonders? Having done it all – blitzing, cold calling and my Mirror approach – I can tell you from the bird's eye, long-term view, which you must have if you are to sustain a long-term business – the quantitative difference in the actual prospects turned clients and the qualitative difference in their value between the two approaches is staggering! It is the "how did you do that?" magic.

So, here is why to move beyond cold calling and blitzing, but now why Mirror Appointment Setting?

First, to understand why Mirror Appointment Setting is so much more successful, you need to let go of your concept of "telemarketing" all together, and move your mind back up to just marketing, with the phone being just one of your (less expensive) marketing tools.

The rule of thumb is that it takes five impressions before you gain a prospective client's attention or "retention," meaning after a minimum of five impressions, (and they must be positive impressions, by the way) our wiring allows us to associate positive impressions with their source (Wikipedia, 2013). This is an age-old adage that still proves true time and again today (MecLabs, 2013; Atlas Institute, 2013; Singh, Niseeth, 2013).

Why wouldn't using the phone as a marketing tool be any different? Think of it this way – the first four impressions, positive or not, are just an interruption. It is only after five positive impressions that a prospective client's mind becomes receptive to your message and the possibility of doing business with you.

Make sense why cold calling and blitzing is always viewed as an abrasive interruption? There are the rare exceptions when you luck out, and the prospect is currently "in the market" (your "one-hit-wonders") for whatever you're selling, but to make sure you're leaving nothing on the table, you don't ever want to be an interruption -- you want to be a prospect's ally always.

You also want to weave phone and email together as marketing tools, whenever possible, providing multiple impression avenues. If you want to win over as many prospects as possible in the long run, you need to be patient, layering your positive impressions over and over and over again. This is no place for "wham, bam, thank you ma'am!" It is simply how we all are hard-wired. I don't need to reiterate the biological/psychological research here (Charny,1966; Kendon,1970; LaFrance, 1979, 1985; Scheflen, 1964) .

Honoring the five impressions rule of thumb answers the first why of Mirror Appointment Setting. Deciding that you're in business for the duration and accepting that it takes layers of positive marketing impressions to convert every prospect possible into a valued, long-term client. But five impressions is not the whole why -- they do have to be perceived as positive impressions by your prospect and you still have to transform a "stranger encounter" into an "alliance."

We've looked in the Mirror and recognized that this is how we all operate, now it's time to look in the Mirror and dig deep into The Golden Rule and that self-reflective accountability I've spoken of to really understand why Mirror Appointment Setting will land you at your destination in building the maximum number of long-term "prospect relationships." This is where you take another significant step in creating an even wider "how did you do that?" competitive margin.

You could send your prospect five emails to gain their receptivity, but how many equally compelling marketing emails are they receiving? Delete. But if they receive an introduction email, then a call, or voicemail from you, according to the unwritten human cultural script, you have demonstrated you are invested and you have properly introduced yourself. Then if you can truly transform your intent completely to servicing their WIFM (What's In It For Me!), which comes through in the tone of your voice and the words you choose, then it is only a matter of time before, as their ally in getting their [put in your product/service] needs met, you convert them from a prospect to a client.

You see, while you may be able to apply some degree of the more surface "mirroring" technique we learned in years of sales training to perhaps tone, the shallowness of this approach is laid bare on the phone. You'll need to actually stare deeply into the Golden Rule Mirror to pull off Mirror Appointment Setting, you'll need to actually MEAN IT in the substance of voice and word. Can you do it?

This is where looking in the Mirror at your self-reflective accountability comes in. Can you be real to the core in placing your prospect's WIFM before your own? Do you believe? Can you really see how doing this will lead to your ultimate success? This is what you would wish for were the roles reversed. Hopefully, the light just went on.

How To Do Mirror Appointment Setting Step-By-Step

Part 1 – Mirror Appointment Setting Set-Up

Here's What You'll Need:

- ➤ Top Flight Mirror Marketers
- ➤ Customized Scripts:
  - Q Script (gathering Intel from receptionists only to qualify leads)
  - DM Script (speaking to the decision maker)
- ➤ Marketing Email(s)
  (These three will be addressed in detail in Part II – Mirror Hiring, and Part III Mirror Marketer Training)
- ➤ Comfortable, quiet space
- ➤ Computer(s)
- ➤ Land-line Phone(s)
- ➤ Professional-Quality-Sound Headset(s)
- ➤ Toll Free Number
- ➤ Scrubbed, qualified Lead List in digital format
- ➤ CRM Software with database sorting & scheduling capabilities
- ➤ Email Program

Tools of the Trade

Let's break down your "tools of the trade" list and discuss each in detail. This book is intended for anyone who is setting up an appointment setting program where marketers are hired to set appointments for direct sales staff – whether phone or face-to-face appointments. This is an important distinction, because while sales people who set their own appointments can take the philosophy from this book to heart, I will be writing a different book just for them, because the step-by-step techniques are necessarily different and in my Mirror strategy -- nuance matters.

This book is also intended for companies who are setting up in-house appointment setting programs. Certainly, telecommuting is hot these days with good reason (I'm telecommuting with contracts I currently have on my plate right now!) I will be writing a different book just for setting up telecommuting appointment setting programs. Again, the philosophy applies, but there is another layer of logistics and nuances that apply.

Comfortable, Quiet Space

So, you're in a company and you're setting up an in-house appointment setting program. Now, you may be a one person firm who is hiring one marketer, or a large company who is setting up an entire department. In both cases, marketers need a comfortable, quiet space to call.

This is not only vital for the productivity of the marketer – but I want you to think about the first thing that tips you off that you've received a telemarketing call from a blitzing, "boiler room" call center before the caller says a word! Even with noise-cancelling headsets, I can still hear the room "boiling" and "blitzing" in the background! Click! You do not want this to happen. I cannot emphasize enough how important this is.

With this type of background being heard, your prospect sets their jaw and is either going to hang-up or at least not be willing to really listen to what your marketer has to say. You've shot your chance from the get-go. You literally need to test this aspect when you are setting up. If your marketer calls you and you can hear background noise, it's back to the drawing board – you need to reconfigure until you can hear zero background.

There's the quiet – we also need to address the comfortable. Honestly, my ultimate, over years & years of reconfiguring, would be for every marketer to be able to call from a zero-gravity chair, with their screen projected above them! Sounds like Star Trek, right? Well, I'll soon be there with my set-up because I know the less I have to think about anything but calling the more I can transport to my focus zone, which means maximum results.

In reality, health-wise, everyone doing office work would be better off in a zero-gravity chair. Working in traditional office chairs takes a heavy toll (Cornell, 2013; Herman Miller, 2013). Zero gravity means zero body strain (NASA, 2013). You can forget all about your body (except for lunch and restroom breaks) and channel all of your energy towards your strategizing in each moment.

If you are of the mind-set that this would spoil your marketers – look in the Mirror and imagine yourself making upwards of 150 dials a day, and sending email after email, in your current set up, and not burning out after eight hours. If loungers or recliners with wireless keyboard, mouse & head-set, a side table and projectors beaming computer screens onto the wall in front of your marketers are the closest you can come to this, it is a vast improvement over a typical office set-up.

Call center set-ups are not only "burn-out city" because of the cold-calling and blitzing and hang-ups, the configurations are mind and body numbing in very short order. You're not designing a call center, after all – because you want different results. You are designing for long-term, sustainable marketer retention and productivity. If you create the design I'm recommending, you should see your marketers feeling valued, able to perform their work comfortably and efficiently for eight hours-a-day, and even viewing their work with you as their career.

Computers

Which CRM (Client Relationship Management software, which we'll discuss shortly) you decide to use sets the minimum parameters for the computer your marketers will need. But as mentioned above, I recommend that you use projectors to beam computer screens onto walls or ceilings or white screens that free the marketer from being confined to a traditional desktop computer and chair. Being on the phone for an entire eight hours is beyond grueling in that type of a set-up. With a wireless keyboard, wireless mouse, wireless head-set, side table and projectors replacing the need to have a screen on a desk, you can set up your marketers for maximum productivity.

Land-Line Phones

It is getting more and more tempting to use "internet" phones, but as of this writing, the quality is just not yet where it needs to be for the professional set-up you desire. This is one of the important nuances in my Mirror approach. You want to present yourself as professionally as you can to your prospects. I've tried the "internet" phones, and so far, they are unacceptable because, even with a high quality headset, prospect feedback is that you sound like you have them on speaker phone. CEOs get to use speaker phone – marketers – not so much.

I had to switch back to land-line service with an unlimited long distance calling package and a commercial-level office phone with a professional sound quality headset. Again, test this. A phone call to you from your Mirror Marketer should be crystal clear.

There are enough problems with prospects' phone lines – make sure none of the sound problems are on your end. You know the saying – you never get a second chance to make a first impression. Sound impeccable.

Professional Sound Head-set

Scrimping on head-set quality, or trying (God forbid) to have your Mirror Marketers use the handset, is setting yourself up for a train wreck and a very high marketer burn-out. Asking a marketer to use a handset is like asking them to drain a lake with a slotted spoon. Again, just imagine yourself making upwards of 150 dials a day, scrunching the handset between your ear and shoulder to free up your hands to type. You may not even make it to eight hours. Invest in quality head-set/ phone systems and make sure they have a good warranty. I have experienced even high quality head-set microphones dying on me. With the warranty, I can quickly get them replaced. And we discussed the importance of your head-set's sound quality.

It is also best to have a head-set/phone system with mute capabilities, and wireless, if possible. Think back to a time when you called a business and were subjected to a whole side conversation while you were waiting – not very professional. Never expose your prospects to your backstage. Your process needs to be seamless -- a front-stage "performance" from end to end.

Toll-Free Number

A defining piece of my Mirror strategy is to provide prospects with a call back number. If you are truly interested in creating long-term relationships with your prospects to eventually convert them to valued clients, then you're willing to run the race, no matter the length. This one item sets you apart and moves you beyond cold-calling and blitzing.

Do prospects call back often? No. But the point is you offered. You have expressed to them, by offering your number for them to call you back, you are interested in doing what it takes to create a real relationship with them on their terms. You are being genuine and open. It is like opening yourself up and extending your hand to shake their hand, which first began as a gesture of trust – actually, a willingness to be transparent that you were not carrying a weapon (Wikipedia, 2013). In Mirror phone marketing, you "shake hands" by offering them a way to call you back, toll-free (an absolute, rather than a courtesy – they must be able to call you for free).

Cold-calling and blitzing believers might gasp at the thought of giving a call back number. They may charge that you've just given up control. Mirror Appointment Setting truly is an alternate paradigm. It is fearless in the sense that letting go, yielding, sharing, enabling your prospect to own the terms of the relationship is not threatening. It is empowering – to your prospect and your Mirror Marketer. It is actually in this nuanced maneuver that you achieve the "Mirror Move," I spoke of in regards to completely surrendering your WIFM to make room for your prospect's WIFM. You've only given up control of getting the "one-hit-wonder" -- and forged the beginnings of a long-term, mutually beneficial relationship with your prospect.

Scrubbed, Qualified Lead List

Obviously, the quality of your lead list is vital to your Mirror Marketer's success. You don't want your Mirror Marketer bogged down with lead list cleaning. You want them to have as fresh a list as possible and stay on top of keeping the database clean, as well as feeding them a constant supply of quality leads. They have a ladder to climb to the Decision Maker as it is, in order to set your appointments. Make that climb as clutter-free as possible by paying attention to the leads you are providing. A stale list is often the demise of the best-intentioned appointment setting program -- and the best marketers.

There are a lot of ways to get lead lists. Rather than detailing all of them here, let's just set your bare minimum lead list parameters, and require any list source to meet them:

> Your Market Area – this seems obvious, but you'd be surprised what I've seen. Be specific.

> "Scrubbed" – meaning the list has been cleaned recently of disconnects/non-working numbers.

> Standard Data – Company name, phone, address, industry type, size – and usually one contact.

> csv file format – most CRMs are able to import lead lists in .csv file format.

This all seems like common sense, but you cannot imagine what I've seen. I'd be much better off just building a list from the year-old yellow pages than a lot of the lists I've come across. I've been contracted when companies hit a wall with their appointment setting programs to come in as a trouble-shooter to clean out the sludge in a database and get the appointment river flowing again. (This is the case with all of the contracts currently on my plate.) I think of it as database gardening. I have to get in there and clean out all of the weeds, put everything in its place, tend to the neglected contacts, and warm everything up to get it humming again.

It amazes me how these companies then act as if I'm magic, once I get the appointments flowing again! They often are blaming the marketer, saying they used to make appointments but just aren't anymore. Yes, it is true that bad hires can really mess up a database. I continue to be astounded at what I find. But I've also come in behind excellent marketers, judging by the quality of their notes, who only need CRM training and a decent lead list. It doesn't help when I call contacts and find out the address is over 20 years old and the contact has been dead for 10. You can turn a great marketer into a bad one with a list like this. It becomes very discouraging. And what a waste! Both the hiring and lead list quality are in the company's control. If neither are quality or tended, you are just throwing good money after bad. Again, look in the Mirror, and imagine your frustration trying to make quality appointments from a 20-year-old list.

Thinking of those great marketers who were fired for not making appointments – yet didn't have proper training or good lead lists to succeed, and thinking of those companies who shot themselves in the foot by not realizing this, inspired me to write this book. While I do enjoy troubleshooting, and I'm good at it – it is no fun when the problems are completely avoidable. Set yourself up to succeed – listen to your Mirror Marketers' list feedback and tend to your lead garden constantly.

CRM - Client Relationship Management Software

The other "magic" companies think I can perform has everything to do with the quality of the CRM. I feel like the Wizard of Oz, putting on this seamless show from behind the CRM curtain. A quality CRM is not only vital in achieving Mirror Appointment Setting, it is vital in navigating from appointment to sale. Whenever I've been the salesperson, or trained the sales staff, I've relied as much on my CRM as when I'm setting the sales appointments. I honestly can't imagine how any sales people can manage without it. It really is one of the top secrets to that "how did you do that?" competitive edge I've enjoyed.

There are a slew of CRMs out there, but, again, rather than detailing them here, let's set your minimum CRM requirements:

- ➤ Search Function – must be able to search by any parameter or keyword.
- ➤ Sorting Function – must be able to sort by any field.
- ➤ Scheduling Function – must be able to schedule contacts for calls, tasks and meetings.
- ➤ Reporting Function – must be able to generate sorted reports.

There can be a lot of other bells and whistles – like email, mail merge, & dialing functions – but walk away if the CRM you are considering doesn't at least have the functions listed above. You can achieve your Mirror Appointment Setting goal if you, at least, have these four functions.

The CRM you end up choosing will also then set your minimum computer requirements. If I get my way, I'll soon be having an affordable, proprietary CRM built to partner with my Mirror Business series that will work on all computer platforms. Over the years, as I've worked with different clients, I've used just about every major CRM there is, as well as some pretty funky & clunky proprietary models. With a CRM being so core to my "high touch" Mirror approach, I look forward to providing my own version as part of a turn-key package.

We'll be getting into more detail than you probably ever wanted to know about maximizing a CRM, towards your goal of building long-term prospect relationships, when we turn towards step-by-step training for your Mirror Marketers.

Email Program

Depending on which CRM you choose, an email program may or may not be integrated into the software. If your CRM does not contain an integrated email program, you'll need a stand-alone program. You don't need anything fancy – just one that works.

The basic standards achieved by most email programs will serve your purpose. Your Mirror Marketers just need to be able to quickly and efficiently email prospects marketing materials. It is handy when you have an email program that can alert the marketer they have received an email. Receptivity and quick response times move you mountains beyond cold-calling and blitzing with your prospects. That your Mirror Marketers respond in real time cements your dedication to a real relationship.

Customized Scripts & Email Marketing Materials

While I will address your Mirror Marketers' phone scripts in detail in **Part III -Mirror Marketer Training,** I want to provide just an overview from a company/manager's perspective here.

We take another huge step beyond cold-calling and blitzing toward Mirror Appointment Setting when it comes to scripts and email marketing. Usually, in a cold-calling/blitzing approach, you are not taking the time to do email marketing. In most cold-calling/blitzing contexts, your scripts are also very aggressive and designed to "take no prisoners -- get the appointment." You certainly are not interested in providing call backs at a more convenient time.

This is perhaps the most significant delineation we make between what has come to be known as "telemarketing," which includes cold-calling and blitzing, and moving towards "marketing via phone/email." We will deal in probably more detail than you ever wanted to know once we are training your Mirror Marketers step-by-step in the section to come, because there are so many nuances that really matter and set your Mirror Marketers apart. I am going to give you a taste here of the difference, though, so you can see where we're headed. Compare this phrasing to what you've heard as a victim of cold-calling/blitzing and you immediately feel the difference:

Mirror Qualifying Script (vs. cold-calling)

Prospect: *"Metrotek, this is Sandra, how may I help you?"*

Mirror Marketer: *"Hi Sandra, I'm hoping you can. This is Sue over at John Abbot's office, and I was first, trying to reach your benefits person, and second, so I don't waste their time, trying to verify your renewal date if you knew it?"*

Prospect: *"Hmm, well (usually a laugh) I'm sorry, I have no idea when the renewal date is, Donna handles that, let me transfer you."*

I'm almost always transferred to the decision maker, where a traditional cold-call script is more likely to be screened and declined or hung-up on by the receptionist. Why? There are several reasons packed into these two sentences. First, it is simple and to the point like a serious, professional call would be (looking in the Mirror, like the kind of professional call you would like and expect to receive) – no fluff, no cold-call red flags. Second, what cold-caller/blitzer has ever stated they care about not wasting the decision maker's time? None that I've ever seen or experienced!

The fact is, the receptionist needs to feel that you are qualifying them just as much as they are qualifying you – and you are. If you have qualifications like number of employees to even set an appointment, you want to know that right up front and you want to ask the receptionist in a way that lets them know you are not willing to go any further in the call without knowing, as you don't want to waste your time or theirs. If they don't know the answer to your qualifying question, they usually greatly appreciate that you are trying not to waste anyone's time, and will transfer you to the decision maker, or ask someone who knows. You are truly a breath of fresh air in comparison to everyone else.

If you have a product or service, like say insurance, that is tied to a renewal time-frame, then you want to qualify this if you can right up front, because not honoring this renewal time-frame will only place you back in the "blitzers don't care" ocean with all of the other telemarketers when you're trying to set yourself apart. And it truly is a waste of your time to call when your annually renewed/purchased product or service is not currently on the company's radar.

Qualify, if you can with the receptionist, to determine this information before attempting to speak to the decision maker. I have asked the receptionist to help me, but more importantly, I have asked the receptionist to help me not waste the decision maker's time. You are also careful to say "over at" to let them know you are local. Stating "John Abbot's office" to the receptionist rather than the company name, communicates that you are his assistant – that you are like them -- administrative staff on the same level as the receptionist you are calling. There is no gimmick – it is genuine. And if you were the receptionist or the decision maker, this is how you would want to be treated, right? So there you have it – a Mirror qualifying approach to directly replace cold-calling.

Mirror Decision Maker Script (vs. cold call sales pitch)

You then take it a step further with your MIRROR DECISION MAKER SCRIPT (vs. Big Cold-Call Sales Pitch). Here's a sample:

Marketer: *"Hi Donna, this is Sue over at John Abbott's office, Abbott & Associates in Hanover. John asked me to give you a call. We weren't sure when you renew your benefits. John was hoping to provide you with a benefits comparison to see if we're a fit, if you were open to that."*

Donna: *"Well, we just renewed last month, March 1st, and we're happy with our current broker."*

Marketer: *"No worries! Is it all right if we touch base next year, just to make sure you're still okay?"*

Donna: *"Sure! You never know!"*

So where's the big sales pitch? You're right – there isn't one. Why? That's what I want to know – why?! The receptionist wasn't able to provide you with the renewal date, so you are letting the decision maker know that you are qualifying, and being thoughtful about whether benefits are currently on her radar. It is like saying, which we all appreciate – "is this a good time?" Again, looking in the Mirror, this is how you would like to be treated and have your time respected, right?

She also threw you an objection that they are happy with their broker. You addressed it in your request to touch base at the appropriate time next year when you offered to provide her a "service call" to "make sure her needs are still being met," which is entirely different than trying to close her on an appointment at the wrong time of year, even though she's happy with her current broker, no matter what she says.

You have made positive impression number one. You have not only proven that you are listening to her, you are taking that a step further by offering to provide her with the service of calling back at the appropriate time to ensure her WIFM is "still" being fulfilled by her current broker, letting her know you are willing to invest the time to wait in the wings and court her business. You have just successfully formed an alliance with your prospect.

Now, you schedule her for next year, begin to add in an email marketing layer leading up to that time, and then follow-up as promised. At that time, when her head is in the benefits game – you then have a window to introduce your quick USP (unique selling point) that might compel her to offer you the opportunity to compete with her current broker. If she once again states they're staying put, you once again, without blinking, say the same request to "touch base" next year, continuing to show your dedication to continuing your alliance with her of making sure her needs are being met -- layering, layering, layering – positive impression upon positive impression.

All of the die-hard cold-callers and blitzers are probably shuddering at this point, or thinking I'm weak – or -- maybe they're not. I've been there, and I'd much rather be here. And rest assured, the long-term results provide the evidence that everyone should be. This is where the "rubber meets the road."

We're at the conclusion of Part I, and you now have what you need to set-up your Mirror Appointment Setting program.

Part II is ready to focus on your most important asset in your program – your stellar marketers. I will address how to hire the best Mirror Marketers, and then, in Part III, it's time for me to take your Mirror Marketers directly by the hand and dig deep into their training, step-by-detailed-step!

Part II – Mirror Marketer Hiring

You have everything in place to put your Mirror Appointment Setting program to work for you. Now where are you going to find the best Mirror Marketers to hire? Are you going to look for marketers with cold-calling/blitzing experience? Or should you look for marketers who have had nothing to do with cold-calling/blitzing/telemarketing?

My favorite phrase when it comes to making thoughtful decisions is: "it depends." This phrase is also part of my Mirror approach, because decisions made with a lot of reflection and then self-reflection are, in my experience, almost always the best decisions. Whenever you make snap judgments based on generalizations without examining each particular situation – or, in this case, each particular candidate – you often miss opportunity. For instance, I've cold-called, blitzed and done just about every angle of telemarketing you can imagine – so will you "file 13" my resume? See what I mean?

But you do need a method to find the best Mirror Marketers so let's think about where applying my Mirror approach to hiring would take us. Honestly, traditional hiring models of stating job requirements and then trying to figure out who is really telling the truth about being a match with those requirements based on their resume is not likely to uncover your Mirror Marketers.

Everyone can tailor their resume to exactly match your job requirements when you're hiring for the "soft skills" necessary for Mirror Appointment Setting. The position doesn't require a certain certificate or certain degree that you can scan for, and, as I pointed out, having or not having previous cold-calling/blitzing/telemarketing skills is not going to enable you to discern whether that candidate is a Mirror Marketer. Some might suggest the standard personality tests, but these tests are still too vague to tease out the Mirror skills we're looking for. So what to do?

You first need to realize that the most fundamental Mirror "skill" you're looking for is not really a skill at all. It is actually a candidate's "way of seeing the world" and their "modus operandi" that you are trying to substantiate. In a nutshell, you must be able to determine whether or not a candidate possesses and more importantly, OPERATES, on a fundamental belief in the Golden Rule. If they do, and they possess the other initial "surface" ingredients needed like a smiling voice, a "gracious-in-the-face-of-pressure/rejection" demeanor, professional speaking & writing ability, 45+ wpm typing ability, and strategic marketing skills, then we can train them on the rest of the skill-sets they need to be a great Mirror Marketer -- if they don't, we need to pass.

I can guarantee you, those candidates who have cold-called/blitzed and who do operate on a fundamental belief in the Golden Rule inevitably feel a tangible conflict in doing so. You find that candidate, and you've likely found the initial ingredients needed to be a Mirror Marketer.

In fact, if you were looking for a pool of potential Mirror marketers, you actually might find them among "failed" cold-callers/blitzers, but this approach is risky because you have to determine why they failed. You have to try to figure out if it was from the biggy reason – fear-of-rejection -- or actually from a "Golden Rule" conflict -- feeling the cold call/blitz method creates a direct conflict with their Golden Rule foundation, and being put in a position to treat others in a way they would not want to be treated creates an untenable situation for them.

But then, we're back to trying to generalize, which is dangerous territory in trying to find the best Mirror Marketers.

There is a more precise method. Broaden your scope back to all of those candidates that first pass a "smiling voice" phone test, then you need to be willing to create what I call a Qualitative Scenario Survey. Qualitative formats are always more work than quantitative multiple choice formats – but it is well worth it.

Candidates are always trying to tell you what you want to hear to get the job – through their resume, personality multiple choice tests, or standard interview questions. Recognizing this, take the time to devise a hiring tool tailored for the particular position to make certain you can sift out those Mirror qualities you are looking for.

The Mirror Hiring Process looks like this:

➢ Create your "hard skills" job requirements to include:
- pleasant/professional-sounding phone voice
- professional speaking & writing ability
- 45 wpm typing ability
- strategic marketing skills
- excellent attention to details

➢ Create your "preferred" list to include:
- previous successful B2B appointment setting experience
- previous CRM (list your preferred software if you'd like) experience preferred

➢ Cull resumes to your short list

➢ Request short-listed candidates perform a call-in recorded voice test or a brief phone interview

> ➤ Successful voice-tested candidates then perform your qualitative Scenario Survey

Candidates' answers to your Scenario Survey (our back-stage title – to your candidates, it is simply your "application") enables you to determine their professional level writing skills, typing skills, strategic marketing skills, attention to detail – but most importantly, the substance of their content enables you to identify those Golden Rule-oriented Mirror Marketers.

The $64,000 question at this point is what questions do you ask on the Scenario Survey, right? The best Scenario Survey will be tailored to your particular business and position. But let's see if we can frame some questions to be customized and included in your Scenario Survey.

Qualitative Scenario Survey

When it comes to designing the questions for your Scenario Survey, (application) you need to think about not only what you'll ask – but why. I'll give you a list of general questions for you to customize, then tell you why.

Suggested questions to include:

> ➤ Receptionist:

- You have reached the receptionist, and you need to determine who makes decisions regarding (your product/service). What will you say?
- The receptionist screens your call – "what is this regarding?" What will you say?
- The receptionist screens your call – "are they expecting your call?" What will you say?
- The receptionist screens your call – "are we currently doing business with you?" What will you say?

- The receptionist tries to take a message, saying they'll call if interested. What will you say?
- The receptionist states they are not interested at this time and hangs-up. What will you do?

➢ Decision Maker:

- You have been transferred to the (your product/service) decision maker and your goal is to set an appointment for (your company's) sales agent. What will you say?
- The decision maker says they're happy with their current (your product/service) provider. What will you say?
- The decision maker asks you to send them an information email, and they'll call if interested. What will you say?
- The decision maker asks you to call back next week. What will you say?
- The decision maker asks you to have (your sales agent) provide a (your product/service) quote by email/phone. What will you say?
- The decision maker states that they are not the final decision maker, but that their process is for the sales agent to meet with them first, then they present the (your product/service) proposal for the final decision. What will you say?
- The decision maker asks you to provide the prices for (your product/service), that they don't have time to meet with (your sales agent). What will you say?
- The decision maker says they are not interested and hangs up. What will you do?

➢ Strategic Marketing Skills:

- You've been given a new database of contacts, and you are responsible for creating the status IDs (ex. "lead," "prospect"). Thinking about the progression from new lead to appointment, what status IDs will you create?

- Thinking about your Status IDs, which group of contacts will you call during lunch?

- You've called a contact and the greeting announces a different business name than the one listed. What will you do?

- You are speaking to a prospect who wants to set an appointment, but they let you know they can't remember when a meeting is that might conflict with the proposed appointment time. What will you do?

- You are speaking to a prospect who wants to set an appointment six months from now, when will you schedule your call back?

- You call a contact and reach a recording stating the number you've called is "no longer in service." What will you do?

- You've reached a doctor's office and been given permission to email information and you're told the doctor will call you if she's interested. Will you schedule this prospect for follow-up? Please explain why or why not.

- You've reached a contact stating decisions regarding (your product/service) are made outside of your market area. What will you do?

- You've reached a greeting that gives the decision maker's cell phone number for emergencies. What will you do and why?

- You've reached a medical clinic and they state they are owned by the hospital. What do you do?
- You've reached a decision maker who tells you "do not call." What do you do?

Now the Why

All of the answers to all of the questions, as I mentioned, help you to determine the candidate's professional writing skill level, typing skills, strategic marketing skills, and attention to detail. Then the "Receptionist" questions give you a sense of how they view the receptionist's role in their success, whether they are "qualifiers," or run-of-the-mill cold-callers, and how they handle "rejection." The "Decision Maker" questions give you a sense of how confident they are when they ask for the appointment, how they handle rejection, and if they are "planters," meaning they know to always attempt to plant a seed for a future follow-up, or "players" (run-of-the-mill blitzers). The Strategic Marketing questions give you a sense of their "in-the-moment" strategic-thinking skills and paint a picture of how they manage prospect relationships in the CRM.

Now, how do you tease out the Mirror Marketer qualities, the Golden Rule-orientation, those self-reflective assets? You look at the phrasing and the word choices they are making when writing what they would say in each instance – do their choices convey a fundamental respect for your prospects and their receptionists? Can you see a gracious demeanor displayed in how they respond to rejection? Do all of their answers display a big-picture, long-term perspective that suggests they understand the importance of creating a sustainable alliance in each and every situation with every lead possible? If you can say yes to these three questions, you've likely found your Mirror marketers! Whew! Hire them!

Compensation

I cannot move on until I at least touch on compensation for your Mirror Marketers. Honestly, if you do this right, you could have Mirror Marketers with you for life! Trouble-shooting, I've come in behind great marketers who were let go for completely avoidable reasons – it's the company who lost out. They were not either properly training the marketer in maximizing the CRM database or they were not providing "live" lead lists. I see the same happening when it comes to compensation. I am, quite frankly, appalled when I scan appointment setting jobs and see what companies are trying to get away with paying marketers.

All I can say is – you get what you pay for. If you want to hire a kid with no college education right out of high school, who is still living at home, go ahead. You may luck out and get a natural Mirror Marketer, but it is not likely. And if you do, they will leave as soon as they need to make a real living. And then you've set yourself up to be a revolving door. You've set your position up to be just on the way to something better. If you only calculate your HR costs alone of this approach, you'll quickly see it is not sustainable, and certainly not in line with my Mirror Business Strategies.

In order to really compensate Mirror Marketers fairly, you cannot compare them to telemarketers working in a call center "way station." A much better formula is to know what it costs you to get a client in each of the ways you currently acquire clients. For instance, how much media marketing dollars do you have to spend to acquire each new client. Do this with each approach you currently use in your business. Then look at what your entire Mirror Appointment Setting program costs you.

You probably already crunched these numbers prior to making the decision to maximize the phone and email as a marketing tool, right? Comparatively speaking, it is very cost efficient. Then you need to factor in the quality and long-term potential of clients acquired through Mirror Appointment Setting, which make those clients – and this approach -- more valuable than almost any other form of marketing. You'll be much closer to what you should be paying Mirror Marketers to acquire & maintain long-term clients for you.

To bring this point home, drill it down and divide up a direct sales agent's time with your company. If that sales person is on their own from A-Z, what percentage of their time do they spend on making a sale, what percentage of their time do they spend going on appointments, and what percentage of their time do they spend prospecting for appointments? We all know the answer is something like 5% / 10% / 85%!

If your sales agents could spend all of their time on the first two – going on appointments and making sales -- how much more profitable would your company be? So if your Mirror Marketers are freeing up 85% of sales agents' time, how much do you think they are worth? Ultimately, remember, all you have to do is look in the Mirror, do that self-reflection and honestly ask yourself in light of this, what compensation package would keep you on as a Mirror Marketer.

You have your Mirror Appointment Setting program all set-up, you've hired your Mirror Marketers – now it's time to turn them over to me in Part III to provide them with their in-depth Mirror Marketer Training. Realize that if you continue reading, the training section is written to the Mirror Marketer, but necessarily repeats sections you've already read in the manager section, since we're starting from square one to train your new Mirror

Marketers, setting their feet on a solid Mirror Appointment Setting foundation. Here we go!

Part III – Mirror Marketer Training

Congratulations! You've made the Mirror Marketer Team! Now what?

Well, first, before we dig into the details, let's talk about what Mirror Appointment Setting means. You're here because you believe in creating long-term prospect relationships – that's right, I said prospect, the step before becoming a client. It takes patience and perseverance – and you've got oodles. You believe what goes around comes around in everything you say and do, and you are dedicated to leaving next to nothing on the table when it comes to long cycle prospect-to-client conversions. You relish turning all those prospects left-behind, by cold-callers and blitzers blowing through, into life-long clients! You savor convincing former clients to rejoin your company's fold. The Golden Rule is just how you roll and you're in it for the long haul.

The Mirror Appointment Setting philosophy recognizes the age-old marketing rule of thumb that it takes at least five positive impressions before we are even willing to consider a buying decision. Welcome to a new way to think of using a phone and email to get in prospects' door. You are marketers, and even though the phone is your primary marketing tool, you are quite different from what we think of as telemarketers. Instead of cold-calling, you are qualifying. Instead of blitzing, you are following up till the cows come home!

Some of you may have previous CRM (client relationship management software) experience and some of you may not. We're not going to leave anything to chance – we'll assume we're all starting from square zero. Even if you have previous CRM experience, you likely will find that this Mirror approach goes much deeper in maximizing a CRM then you ever have before.

I'm going to approach this step-by-step, walking you through each detail.

Because my Mirror approach is applying layer upon layer of positive marketing impressions, we'll keep layering your training, too, giving you more and more nuanced layers to help you succeed in making those appointments – against all odds! Let's get started!

Review the set-up list in Part I. I am going forward, assuming you have been provided with all of these tools. That being said, it's time to tailor your marketing tools.

Email Signature

You'll be sending a lot of marketing emails to achieve those layered positive impressions, so we need to customize your email signature. You'll need to figure out how to set-up your signature in your particular email program. Once you do, I recommend you set-up the following format:

(Your Name)
Assistant
(Phone with direct extension)
(Email Address)
(Company Website)

Why? Because you want your signature to convey that you work in a professional office setting, that you are in an assistant capacity-which makes you approachable for the administrative staff and decision makers you will be calling, and that you are accessible with a direct extension and email.

Voicemail Greeting

You'll want to record a professional and to-the-point, but friendly, voice mail greeting, something like:

"This is (Your Name), I am either on the phone or away from my desk. Please leave your name, number and message and I'll return your call as soon as I can. Thank you."

Why? You want to make sure and skip any "marketing fluff" or "sales red flags" in your greeting. Make it plain and simple – all business but smiling.

Paper Appointment Calendar

Even though you will be scheduling appointments in your CRM and possibly on a networked calendar, depending on how your company has the sales appointment schedule set up, I still recommend you have a paper calendar right in front of you (as well as a small notepad). I often set appointments for several sales agents at once, so I have a "key" and each agent has an assigned number:

Julie – 1
Michael – 2
Andrew – 3
Scott - 4

That way, all I need to do is place the agent's corresponding number in the appointment I am setting for them IN PENCIL. Always only use a pencil on your paper calendar – you WILL need to make changes. I use mechanical pencils because they are always sharp. When you are speaking to a prospect on the phone, you want everything to feel streamlined, you can't ask the prospect to wait for you to move from screen to screen, so having the paper calendar, you can see availability at a glance at the same time you are verifying information and typing their details in the CRM.

Your paper calendar is also very motivating! You can see how many appointments you have at any given time. I actually do not use a pre-printed calendar, though you can. I use a stenographer's pad and set it sideways, then draw (with pen) in the timelines (see image below). I can fit a whole month, with the days & dates along the top, and the hours down the left side.

April 2013   Key - Julie-1, Michael-2, Andrew-3, Scott-4

	1	2	3	4	5	8	9	10	11	12	15	16	17	18	19	22	23	24	25	26	29	30
	M	T	W	T	F	M	T	W	T	F	M	T	W	T	F	M	T	W	T	F	M	T
8																						
9																						
10	1																					
10	2																					
10	3																					
10	4																					
11																						
12																						
1																						
2																						
2																						
2																						
2																						
3																						
4																						
5																						
6																						
7																						
8																						

Paper calendar

Create a visual break between weeks, so you can see one week at a glance. On my sample calendar, you'll also notice I have four 10am slots and four 2pm slots. That is because these are the two times I'm always trying to direct appointments to, and if I'm calling for four sales agents, for instance, I have a slot for each at those times. I always direct to 10am first, then offer 2pm. The rest of the times only have one slot because I rarely need to book other than 10am or 2pm. How your company sets up their sales scheduling will determine how you customize your paper calendar. This is just an example for you. Nothing fancy! I always say simple is better.

Email Templates

You'll want to create some email templates for emails you'll send frequently, just to save time. I've found that I have three emails I send often:

- ➢ 1st Appointment Confirmation Email for Prospect
- ➢ New Appointment Email for Sales Agent
- ➢ 2nd Appointment Confirmation Email for Prospect (if you couldn't reach on phone to confirm)

Here is a suggested format for each:

1st Appointment Confirmation

Hi (Prospect's Name),

Thanks for taking the time to speak to my assistant, (Your Name).

I have set aside time for us on (Day, Date, Time) at your office.

My objective is to perform a custom assessment to see if our (Your company product/service) is a fit. I feel we have something of great value, but of course we will need to determine if we're a match.

Should the need arise you can contact me directly at (Sales Agent's phone and direct extension).

Sincerely,

(Sales Agent's Name)
(Sales Agent's Title)

--Your email signature will appear here.

New Appointment Email

"Hi (Sales Agent's Name),

I have scheduled an appointment for you with (Prospect's Name-Title) at (Prospect's Company Name) on (Day, Date, Time).

Hope you're having a great day!

Thanks,"

--your email signature will appear here.

2nd Appointment Confirmation Email

"Hi (Prospect's Name)

This is to confirm our appointment on (Day, Date, Time) at your office.

I look forward to our meeting.

Should the need arise you can contact me directly at (Sales Agent's phone with direct extension).

Sincerely,"

(Sales Agent's Name)
(Sales Agent's Title)

--your email signature will appear here.

Notice that the emails to the prospects are from the sales agent they will be meeting with, again placing you in the assistant role, and providing a personal touch from the sales agent.

You will also have one, and maybe more, marketing emails that you'll send often. We'll address them after we speak about your phone scripts.

Mirror Appointment Setting Phone Scripts

Whether or not you've had previous cold-calling or blitzing experience, you've likely experienced being on the receiving end.

In Mirror Appointment Setting, we take a huge step beyond cold-calling and blitzing when it comes to our phone scripts and email marketing – because our goals of creating long-term prospect relationships, leaving next-to-nothing on the table with long cycle prospect-to-client conversions, and maximizing client retention, quickly diverge after that first call hit. Usually, in a cold-calling/blitzing approach, you are not taking the time to do email marketing. In most cold-calling/blitzing contexts, your scripts are also very aggressive and designed to "take no prisoners -- get the appointment." You certainly are not providing call backs at a more convenient time.

This is perhaps the most significant delineation we make between what has come to be known as "telemarketing," which includes cold-calling and blitzing, and moving towards "marketing via phone/email." We will deal with the what, how and why of your Mirror phone scripts in deep detail, because there are so many nuances that really matter and set you apart as Mirror Marketers.

In order to frame the backdrop for Mirror phone scripts, we need to talk more specifically about the why of Mirror Appointment Setting. This approach has a different goal than traditional telemarketing. Traditional telemarketing, even if you are attempting to just set sales appointments rather than actually sell over the phone, is designed to flash through and harvest the low-hanging fruit.

Mirror Appointment Setting, on the other hand, is designed to continually harvest the entire orchard over time, wasting next to

Mirror Appointment Setting

nothing. Your company is dedicated to harvesting the entire orchard of prospects within their market area in a sustained effort over time, gradually turning nearly all of them into clients. That is why they've implemented a Mirror Appointment Setting program and hired you as a Mirror Marketer.

What does a Mirror have to do with it? The only way to sustain a harvest over time is to create alliances with prospects, continually following up with them on their time table until they are willing to become clients. It's how you would want to be treated, right? There's the key, and a Mirror is my metaphor for reflecting on how to treat others the way you want to be treated – operating from a Golden Rule orientation in everything you say and do regarding your company's prospects.

Yeah – common sense, right? It's true. But how often is it actually being followed? When a telemarketer calls you, 9.9999 times out of 10, you don't feel you're being treated the way you'd like, right? There you have it. Bottom line, we cannot create positive relationships with prospects over time unless we're very careful to treat them the way we would like to be treated from the first moment.

So, every subtle detail of your interactions as Mirror Marketers with prospects is carefully thought through from this perspective, because it is easier said than done. And you must not only focus on treating prospects the way you would like to be treated, you must take it a step further, again using the Mirror metaphor, to self-reflect and literally put the prospect's WIFM (What's In It For Me) ahead of your own. For example, getting permission from a prospect to provide an annual touch base "service call" must override pushing to get an appointment today. That is a monumental shift!

You want to set appointments – but not at the expense of alienating even one prospect. You have been hired because your company believes you are capable of successfully navigating this paradigm shift. If we train you properly, and you implement that training on every single call, prospects' response to you will be refreshing!

You are transformed from being an interruption into being an ally who is going to make sure their needs, in regards to your company's product/service, are being met, day after day, year after year, for as long as it takes, until they are ready to set an appointment. If your company's competition falls short, you will be there, ready and willing to pick up the pieces and get your sales agent out there pronto on an appointment. When done right, your prospects will be asking you to call them back and appreciating that you are willing to. Do you believe me? Here's the proof.

Compare this phrasing to what you've heard on the receiving end of cold-calling/blitzing and you can immediately feel the difference:

| *Mirror Qualifying Script (vs. cold-calling)*

Prospect: *"Metrotek, this is Sandra."*

Mirror Marketer: *"Hi Sandra, I'm hoping you can help me. This is Sue over at John Abbot's office, and I was first, trying to reach your benefits person, and second, so I don't waste their time, was trying to verify your renewal date if you knew it?"*

Prospect: *"Hmm, well (usually a laugh) I'm sorry, I have no idea when the renewal date is, Donna handles that, let me transfer you."*

You'll almost always be transferred to the decision maker, where a traditional cold-call script is more likely to be screened and declined or hung-up on by the receptionist. Why? There are several reasons packed into these two sentences. First, it is simple and to the point like a serious, professional call would be (looking in the Mirror, like the kind of professional call you would like and expect to receive) – no fluff, no cold-call red flags. Second, what cold-caller/blitzer has ever stated they care about not wasting the decision maker's time? None that I've ever seen or experienced!

The fact is, the receptionist needs to feel that you are qualifying them just as much as they are qualifying you – and you are. If you have qualifications your company requires like number of employees to even set an appointment, you want to know that right up front and you want to ask the receptionist in a way that lets them know you are not willing to go any further in the call without knowing, as you don't want to waste your time or theirs. If they don't know the answer to your qualifying question, they usually greatly appreciate that you are trying not to waste anyone's time, and will transfer you to the decision maker, or ask someone who knows. You are truly a breath of fresh air in comparison to everyone else.

If you have a product or service, like say insurance, that is tied to a renewal time-frame, then you want to qualify this, if you can, right up front because not honoring this renewal time-frame will only place you back in the "blitzers don't care" ocean with all of the other telemarketers when you're trying to set yourself apart. And it truly is a waste of your time to call when your annually renewed/purchased product or service is not currently on the company's radar.

Qualify, if you can, with the receptionist, to determine this information before attempting to speak to the decision maker. I have asked the receptionist to help me, but more importantly, I have asked the receptionist to help me not waste the decision maker's time. You are also careful to say "over at" to let them know you are local. Stating "John Abbot's office" to the receptionist rather than the company name, communicates that you are his assistant – that you are like them -- administrative staff on the same level as the receptionist you are calling. There is no gimmick – it is genuine. And if you were the receptionist or the decision maker, this is how you would want to be treated, right? So there you have it – a Mirror qualifying approach to directly replace cold-calling.

| *Mirror Decision Maker Script (vs. cold call sales pitch)*

You then take it a step further with your Mirror Decision Maker Script. Here's a sample:

Marketer: *"Hi Donna, this is Sue over at John Abbott's office, Abbott & Associates in Hanover. John asked me to give you a call. We weren't sure when you renew your benefits. John was hoping to provide you with a benefits comparison to see if we're a fit, if you were open to that."*

Donna: *"Well, we just renewed last month, March 1st, and we're happy with our current broker."*

Marketer: *"No worries! Is it all right if we touch base next year, just to make sure you're still okay?"*

Donna: *"Sure! You never know!"*

So where's the big sales pitch? You're right – there isn't one. Why? That's what I want to know – why?! The receptionist wasn't able to provide you with the renewal date, so you are letting the decision maker know that you are qualifying, and being thoughtful about whether benefits are currently on her radar. It is like saying, which we all appreciate – "is this a good time?"

Again, looking in the Mirror, this is how you would like to be treated and have your time respected, right? She also threw you an objection that they are happy with their broker. You addressed it in your request to touch base at the appropriate time next year when you offered to provide her a "service call" to "make sure her needs are still being met," which is entirely different than trying to close her on an appointment at the wrong time of year, even though she's happy with her current broker, no matter what she says. You have made positive impression number one.

You have not only proven that you are listening to her, you are taking that a step further by offering to provide her with the service of calling back at the appropriate time to ensure her WIFM is "still" being fulfilled by her current broker, letting her know you are willing to invest the time to wait in the wings and court her business. You have just successfully formed an alliance with your prospect.

Now, you schedule her for next year, begin to add in an email marketing layer leading up to that time, and then follow-up as promised. At that time, when her head is in the benefits game – you then have a window to introduce your quick USP (unique selling point) that might compel her to offer you the opportunity to compete with her current broker. If she once again states they're staying put, you once again, without blinking, say, the same request to "touch base" next year, continuing to show your dedication to continuing your alliance with her of making sure her needs are being met -- layering, layering, layering – positive impression upon positive impression.

All of the die-hard cold-callers and blitzers are probably shuddering at this point, or thinking I'm weak – or -- maybe they're not. I've been there, and I'd much rather be here. And rest assured, the long-term results provide the evidence that everyone should be. This is where the "rubber meets the road."

Customizable Mirror Phone Scripts for Receptionists

In Mirror Appointment Setting, you recognize that the receptionist is your most important ally. In contrast to traditional telemarketing, you do not need to view the receptionist as a "gatekeeper" who is trying to keep you out. Honestly, they are just trying to keep telemarketers from interrupting decision makers. It is true that because they are hounded by telemarketers, you'll occasionally find receptionists who are just about in hang up auto pilot and you, too, may get hung up on (same with decision makers).

Patience. Don't take it personal. It is not about you. They are in telemarketer reaction mode. After all, they are trying to run a business and when telemarketers do not respect their time, "click" becomes their automatic reflex. Most receptionists, though, will instantly appreciate your Mirror approach and be helpful. You are not only creating prospect relationships, you are first creating relationships with receptionists and assistants who will go to bat for you when they are appreciated and treated with respect.

As you do Mirror Appointment Setting, you will also come to see that there is a rhythm and flow in your phone scripts. There is also a time limit, and your phone scripts must reflect that. It is subtle, but if you violate that rhythm or time limit you'll likely be hung up on. It is almost an unspoken rule that traditional telemarketing has ignored with expected results. With your Mirror phone scripts, you will be asking for their help in bits over time so as to keep within that rhythm and time-flow. This rhythm and time-frame are really the same as accepted etiquette in our face-to-face interactions. When someone asks in passing, "How are you," you know they don't really want you to explain in detail – and neither would you in their shoes, right? There is a rhythm and time limit – "I'm fine and you?" or "can't complain." It is out of mutual respect (the Golden Rule) that we honor these seemingly subtle, but important, manners.

Here are Mirror scripts you can customize for use with Receptionists:

Mirror Qualifying Script:
"Hi, this is (your name) over at (sales agent's name) office. I'm hoping you can help me. I'm, first, trying to reach your (your product/service handler's title) person and second, so I don't waste their time, I'm trying to verify (your company's #1 qualifier – "if you have at least 5 employees" or "your renewal date" or ?), if you knew." (If they don't know the qualifier) "No worries! Who handles that?"

Mirror Decision Maker's Email Address Request:

Initial Request:
"Hi, this is (your name) over at (sales agent's name) office. I'm hoping you can help me. I'm supposed to email (decision maker's name). Would you have that email so I can send this over?"

After Reach Attempts:
"Hi, this is (your name) over at (sales agent's name) office. I'm hoping you can help me. I've been trying to reach (decision maker's name). Would you happen to have an email for him/her – so I could just send this over?"

Mirror BTTC (best time to call) Script:
    "Hi, this is (your name) over at (sales agent's name) office. I'm hoping you could help me. I've been trying to reach (decision maker's name). Would you know the best time to call?"

Customizable Mirror Scripts for Decision Makers

Mirror Decision Maker Qualifier Script:
    "Hi (decision maker's name), this is (your name) over at (sales agent's name) office, (company name) in (city). (sales agent's name) asked me to give you a call. We weren't sure (qualifier - # employees, renewal date, etc.). (sales agent's name) would like to provide you with a (your product/service) comparison to see if we're a fit, if you're open to that."

Answer Scenarios:
    (Do not qualify) *"Oh. We would really need (qualifier) to go further. Thanks for your time."* (End the call.)

    (Not the right time – ex. just renewed) *"No worries! Is it all right if we touch base for next year?* (Usually will be pleasantly surprised and answer yes.) (If an annual renewal product/service: *"When do you renew so we know the best time to call?"*) *Thank you! Talk to you then!"*

    (Happy) *"That's great! No worries! Is it all right if we touch base in a year, just to make sure your needs are still being met?* (Usually will be pleasantly surprised and answer yes.) *Thank you! Talk to you then!"* (We will use a version of this approach with every objection. Remember, your first goal is to transition to an ally relationship – go with the flow, and get permission to provide a "service call" – you can gauge how solid their objection is and either try to handle the objection once you have that permission with a "by the way," or wait until your next follow-up, when you have earned some "credit" by keeping your promise. We'll deal with objections in much more detail coming up.)

Handling Objections

You're really not ready to handle "solid" objections on the first go-round with decision makers, because you have to respect that rhythm & time flow we spoke of, and there is not enough time to qualify AND handle objections. Remember, your over-riding goal is to receive permission to follow-up again at a future time. For most decision makers, you have not yet earned the right to address their solid objection, and if you push to anyway – click. They assume you're just another rude telemarketer AND you didn't get what you were after, which was their agreement for you to contact them in the future.

Now, you not only have to start over, you have to begin from behind the start line because you now have a negative impression against you. You'll have to pull this decision maker out of your regular rotation and give them some time before you can call again and start over.

There are exceptions to this. Rarely, you'll reach a decision maker who is willing to take more time – they will let you know. This is a "setting-sign" – they may be interested, even though they automatically spilled out their initial objection.

But the reason they now may be interested is because you didn't pounce on their objection. You kept the flow and now they are intrigued. They'll usually ask you questions or go into detail about their situation, which you need to note. Play it out and see where it goes. Are they willing to set an appointment? You can ask again. They'll often say they'd like a call back – so you've now achieved your goal, but you also have a much warmer prospect when you do follow-up with them. Way to go!

Sometimes, you'll reach a decision maker whose objection is "soft" and this is a sign you need to go in for the appointment again, but first address their "soft" objection. An example would be, "I've gotten insurance quotes in the past and they're all the same, why should I bother?"

Hopefully, you have a success story from a previous situation to share, or borrow a colleague's story, if you don't. "You know, I've heard that. Then I was talking to this electrical contractor who said he'd been with the same guy for over 25 years, never getting quotes. When his son came on board he convinced him to get a quote, and he ended up saving $8,300 a year for the same exact insurance, just a different broker! Now he makes sure to get a quote every year!" (True story – feel free to use it!)

The difference between "solid" and "soft" objections is that in order to handle a solid objection, you have to swim against the tide. For instance, the product/service you offer has an annual renewal, and the decision maker just renewed last month. Once you set your follow-up to go with this decision maker's flow, which is his renewal cycle in this case, and as you accumulate layers of positive impressions, you will eventually be able to build enough rapport, and you will have deposited enough "credits" in your prospect relationship account, to overcome this objection.

Soft objections, on the other hand, communicate to you that the decision maker is interested, but wants you to convince them setting an appointment is in their WIFM's (What's In It For Me) best interest, like the example above. I call soft objections an "almost yes." How can you guarantee you know the difference? Ah – you just have to listen. You just have to really listen.

The more you stay focused on listening to what your decision makers are saying, the more you'll be able to get to where you automatically know which kind of objection you're dealing with and where to go with it. One still goes with the flow (soft) and one would require a break in the flow (solid). Don't break the flow! You'll be amazed at your decision maker's response when you don't break the flow – they'll find you refreshing. It is astounding. When you don't break the flow, oddly enough, they open the door to you and agree to future contact.

Why? Look in the Mirror, and realize we all want to be heard, and have what we say acknowledged. That's what you've done. You've proven that you've heard and acknowledged what your decision maker said, and most importantly, that you respect their wishes, asking them for permission to contact them at a future time.

I know, this flies in the face of what you may have learned cold-calling and blitzing, and what you may have heard about sales in general. Over 30 years as a business development specialist focused in sales and marketing, I've yet to meet those people cold-call/blitz/slick willy sales training speaks of who want to be bullied and beaten down into relenting. It is such a short-sighted view. All we have to do is look in the Mirror to know they don't exist. Just treat every receptionist and decision-maker the way you would want to be treated in everything you say and do, and you'll find exceptional success!

When it comes to handling objections, I've discussed types of objections in broad strokes and told you when to handle them, in general. It is important to understand what the common objections for your company's products/services are, and what to say to handle those specific objections. I'll need your company to provide you with this information.

We've now addressed your phone scripts and the nuances of accomplishing Mirror Appointment Setting. Amazing how much the details matter in what you say and how you say it, right? Perception is everything, especially with first impressions. Do the details seem overwhelming? They don't need to be. You have a tried and true compass – the Mirror. All you really have to do to stay on course is keep looking in the Mirror, and treating everyone the way you would want to be treated. If you succeed in doing this one thing until you can put the rest of the details into play, you'll be leagues ahead of your competition.

Email Marketing

You've learned how to layer positive impressions with your phone scripts. We now turn to adding impact to those phone layers with email marketing. While email is new, the idea of sending a letter of introduction is ancient – but it still applies! Going back to those unwritten cultural scripts, it is the respectful and appropriate thing to do, followed-up with a call. Traditional telemarketing isn't going to take the time, so with one click of the "send" button, you've established a huge advantage, setting you apart as a Mirror Marketer from the sea of telemarketers.

You are also appealing to our human attention physiology with an alternate positive impression format. With that marketing rule of thumb that it takes at least five positive impressions before you can get on your prospects' attention radar, presenting impressions via multiple media formats enriches your total impression once you've made it in. It also communicates to your prospect that you are invested in getting their attention – that you are serious about wanting to create a long-term relationship with them, and earning their business.

You first need at least one email marketing piece introducing your company, and your product/service. It would be best to have just one to begin with, and you'll just customize the first couple of sentences to fit each situation. The body of the email will be specific to your company, and there needs to be a statement that you will be contacting them, as well as yours and the sales agent's contact information at the end, but I will address different situations and customizations for the introduction -- the first couple of sentences.

First Contact after getting email address from Receptionist – Qualifying

Hi (Decision Maker's name),

(receptionist's name) spoke to my assistant, (your name). We weren't sure when you (renew/consider your product/service).

Body. (Company information with USP-unique selling proposition)

(your name) will contact you to set up a convenient time for us to talk personally. I look forward to speaking with you to discuss how (your company) can improve your (product/service experience).

Thank you for your time and consideration and I look forward to speaking with you soon. If you have any questions, please contact us at (your phone number with direct extension) or you can contact me directly at (sales agent's phone number with direct extension).

Sincerely,

(Sales Agent's Name)
(Sales Agent's Title)

--Your email signature will appear here.

Follow-up Email (Still Qualifying)

Hi (Decision Maker's name),

My assistant, (your name) tried to reach you. We weren't sure when you (renew/consider your product/service).

Body. (Company information with USP-unique selling proposition)

(your name) will contact you to set up a convenient time for us to talk personally. I look forward to speaking with you to discuss how (your company) can improve your (product/service experience).

Thank you for your time and consideration and I look forward to speaking with you soon. If you have any questions, please contact us at (your phone number with direct extension) or you can contact me directly at (sales agent's phone number with direct extension).

Sincerely,

(Sales Agent's Name)
(Sales Agent's Title)

--Your email signature will appear here.

1st Contact Prior to Scheduled Follow-Up on Annual Schedule or Renewal Date

Hi (Decision Maker's name),

We weren't sure when you begin to review. From previous conversations, we noted you are set for a (renewal/purchase schedule) with your (product/service). My assistant, (your name) will contact you as we move closer.

Body. (Company information with USP-unique selling proposition) (your name) will contact you to set up a convenient time for us to talk personally. I look forward to speaking with you to discuss how (your company) can improve your (product/service experience).

Thank you for your time and consideration and I look forward to speaking with you soon. If you have any questions, please contact us at (your phone number with direct extension) or you can contact me directly at (sales agent's phone number with direct extension).

Sincerely,

(Sales Agent's Name)
(Sales Agent's Title)

--Your email signature will appear here.

1ˢᵗ Contact at One Year Agreed Scheduled Follow-Up Date

Hi (Decision Maker's name),

From previous conversations, we had a note to contact you in (month). My assistant, (your name) is following up as promised.

Body. (Company information with USP-unique selling proposition)

(your name) will contact you to set up a convenient time for us to talk personally. I look forward to speaking with you to discuss how (your company) can improve your (product/service experience).

Thank you for your time and consideration and I look forward to speaking with you soon. If you have any questions, please contact us at (your phone number with direct extension) or you can contact me directly at (sales agent's phone number with direct extension).

Sincerely,

(Sales Agent's Name)
(Sales Agent's Title)

--Your email signature will appear here.

These marketing email templates will help you with the most common situations you will encounter. Of course, your company's particular situation and product/service may require additional customizations. You do want to "keep it simple silly" (KISS) with your marketing emails.

It is easy to get too fancy and forget that these emails are complementing your phone efforts. Making enough dials a day is your most important function because, while it occasionally happens that you'll have a decision maker willing to set an appointment from an email (I've probably had three in the last year), the primary function of these marketing emails is to act as a letter of introduction prior to your first phone call. The phone is where you'll set more than 99% of your appointments.

If your company has one or two more pieces that are simple and informational, that meet all of the above requirements for our Mirror marketing emails, you can rotate them in at different follow-up points. Again, remember, the reasons we are doing marketing emails are to achieve the following:

- a polite letter of introduction
- a written positive impression
- a "soft" impression prior to your phone call
- proof that you are invested in creating a prospect relationship

We've now wrapped up a large portion of your Mirror Marketer set-up. There is still a very important set-up process ahead of us – your CRM (Client Relationship Management system).

Mirror Appointment Setting CRM Set-Up

Are you ready to go real deep? It is necessary because your Mirror CRM is your lean, mean secret client-maker machine! Everything we've discussed so far has focused on you, your words and actions as a Mirror Marketer that set you apart from telemarketers.

The fact is, you wouldn't be able to "under-promise and over-deliver," which should always be your goal, without the technical assistance of your Mirror CRM system. I am assuming your company has provided you with a CRM that has the capabilities required to achieve Mirror Appointment Setting listed in the set-up section, we now need to set it all up for you to use.

We may be stating the obvious at times if you've used CRMs before. If you haven't, we'll lead you step-by-step to make sure you maximize this tool to its fullest potential for Mirror Appointment Setting. If you embrace this training, I bet you'll be thinking of your own streamlining improvements specific to your company in no time!

Since there are several CRMs that meet our requirements, we will be speaking in functional generalities rather than specifics regarding any particular software. Your CRM, at a minimum, needs to have a:

- Search Function – must be able to search by any parameter or keyword.
- Sorting Function – must be able to sort by any field.
- Scheduling Function – must be able to schedule contacts for calls, tasks and meetings.

- Reporting Function – must be able to generate sorted reports.

But let's back up a minute and address the question, just what is a CRM and what is it for? A CRM is either computer software or software in the "cloud," that allows you to store, sort, and schedule the tasks you need to perform to either achieve client relationships or maintain them. It's a fancy address book and calendar rolled into one.

Some of you might remember the paper planners business people use to lug around. Mine contained my entire life – every contact, every appointment, every detail. Thanks to computer databases and calendars, we can manage all of this important information much more efficiently. Being able to manage all of this data in what came to be called CRMs "upped my game" exponentially. I could sustain maintenance of significantly more contacts than ever before. This fact makes your ability to manage hundreds and even thousands of contacts possible.

I've used just about every off-the-shelf CRM, cloud CRMs, and lots of proprietary CRMs my client companies had customized just for them. You can have all kinds of bells and whistles – but I always recommend "keep it simple silly," (KISS) and suggest companies just make sure they purchase a CRM for you to use with a minimum of the above four requirements.

Minimum Functions and Why They Are Necessary

➤ **Search Function** – must be able to search by any parameter or keyword.

- I've been called in to troubleshoot databases after marketers who obviously weren't aware how, or were just too lazy, to search and this turned out to be the single most important factor in salvaging the database, and getting it producing again. How is that important to you? Well, you have to come in after yourself!

- Think of yourself as a different person each day and the "you today" can't remember on which contact the "you of yesterday" wrote that great testimonial in the notes that you could really use today. This is understandable. After all, you're likely managing 150+ contacts each day – who could blame you? If you just remember one keyword from that testimonial, you can likely quickly find it. Searching also enables you to keep your contacts neat and tidy, increasing your efficiency and therefore, your results, which is what it is all about, right?

- Of course, the best approach is to "clean up after yourself" with each and every contact to make sure everything stays very organized – but 150+ dials a day, with fingers flying, you don't always have a chance to, even with best intentions. You also may get a strategic marketing idea from one contact that you realize you can use with certain other contacts – you must be able to search and group those certain other contacts. Searching is obviously so important in most any computer application these days – this is all likely common sense to you.

➢ **Sorting Function** – must be able to sort by any field.

- Sorting is really a type of search. But with sorting, you are looking to group a cluster of contacts all possessing the same identifier. This is so vital! For instance, you want to send a pre-call introduction email to all contacts with a particular renewal or scheduled call back date occurring within the next four months. Sorting allows you to gather those contacts in a list so you can send that email. It also allows you to place contacts in a certain order – alphabetical, by call back date, by title – you name it! If there is a corresponding field or identifier, you can sort by it.

- Think how much time this function saves you.

➢ **Scheduling Function** – must be able to schedule contacts for calls, tasks and meetings.

- You can have all of your contacts neatly organized, but if you can't schedule your follow-up with each contact – it's pointless. And I have had to use CRMs that don't have scheduling – they shouldn't be able to say they're anything more than a contact list. That's all they are if they can't schedule. Scheduling is how you automate your contact management. It is how you exponentially increase your results.

- What is scheduling after all? It is all about timing. Since you are not blitzing, but rather performing Mirror Appointment Setting, the timing is all about your prospects. You can guarantee you will call them back when they ask you to call them back. And it's not on a separate piece of paper somewhere to remind you, or a separate piece of software you have to try to manage, entering contacts in both places – once scheduled in your CRM, you find them automatically popping up on today's follow-up list – Ta! Da! You can guarantee you can call within that precise opportunity window when your prospects' attention is on your company's product/service. It's all about maintaining that rhythm and flow.

- It still amazes me how surprised prospects are that you actually called back when they asked you to! If there is one way to leave other telemarketers or sales agents in the dust, this is it. What better way to communicate to your prospects that you are invested in creating a relationship with them – that you're in it for the long haul! I cannot even quantify the success I've experienced for no other reason than being that person who actually calls them back when they asked. Here's the secret to that success – plain and simple.

➢ **Reporting Function** – must be able to generate sorted reports.

- My number one reason for wanting reports is to look in the Mirror and reflect on how I can improve. I hope it will be yours as well. Reports help me to do that. Your company will want reports, of course, to track your progress, to identify training opportunities, and to formulate their sales projections. But, having said all of that, don't hang your star on reports. They can provide you with a pattern and strategic marketing ideas – but they can also consume way too much time that is better spent hitting rubber to road – making dials.

- Leave the majority of gathering reports to your company and perhaps allow yourself one report to track – which one at any given time depends on which particular area you are trying to monitor and improve. Let this one report be your measuring stick until you reach your goal in that area, then move on to a different report.

- For instance, what results are you getting from your email/phone impression layering campaign? You can create a report of all those contacts you sent a pre-call email to and determine your appointment ratio compared to no pre-call email contacts. Is there a significant difference? Most reporting is more for your company – but is vital to continually providing you with relevant training and constantly polishing your Mirror Appointment Setting system.

Now that we've discussed CRMs in broad strokes, we'll turn to Mirror Marketer customization.

Tailoring Your CRM for Mirror Appointment Setting

I've emphasized how important calling a prospect back when they ask you to call them back is -- how important keeping the rhythm and flow is -- to your success. When you take a long-term vs a "one hit wonder" view, you are layering multiple tasks with hundreds if not thousands of contacts each day. In order to achieve this efficiently, you need to tailor your CRM to assist you. That's what it is for! Maximize your CRM and you maximize your results.

When you stand back and view the process of turning a contact into an appointment, there are several steps you must move a contact through to get them there. You have to be able to keep orchestrating all of the contacts at all of the steps as you gracefully move them all towards client status. As long as your company continues to supply you with fresh contacts, you'll always have a group at each step, flowing them along like a river. Mirror Status IDs are how you pull this off.

Mirror Status IDs

Perhaps the most important step in tailoring your CRM for Mirror Appointment Setting is to set your Contact Status IDs. I'm assuming your company has provided you with a CRM that is loaded with leads for you to call, and that those leads all have standard data - company name, phone, address, industry type, size – and usually one contact, which is often the President/CEO/Owner. So what is a Status ID and why are they important? A Status ID qualifies and categorizes your contacts, enabling you to organize them for easy access.

A "Lead," for instance, is a Status ID, and it is where all contacts begin on their way to becoming a client in Mirror Appointment Setting. But there are steps in between as you move each contact along and opportunities with contacts would fall through the cracks if you weren't able to make certain Status ID distinctions. These nuances are vitally important in Mirror Appointment Setting, and are one of the reasons Mirror Marketers excel above telemarketers who are usually calling out of one big ocean of contacts.

Most CRMs have generic default Status IDs. They'll usually have "Prospect," but in Mirror Appointment Setting, there are several more qualifications on a contact's way to even becoming a prospect.

In the beginning, all of the leads share the same Status ID because you have not yet called them to gather the "intel" to qualify them for the next level on the Status ID "Ladder."

In Mirror Appointment Setting, your Status IDs in alphabetical order look like this:

- Dead=OOB (out of business)
- DNC=do not call
- Disconnected=NIS (not in service) phone is disconnected
- DM=Decision Maker identified
- Duplicate=duplicate lead
- Existing Client=existing client identified
- HOLD-DM hung up; DM will call if interested; seasonal; needs intel; networked leads

- Lead=unreached lead
- Not Qualified=NQ lead is not qualified
- Out of Area=OOA decisions are made outside your market area
- Past Appointment=held appointments
- Phone/Email Appointment=phone/email requests referred to sales team
- Prospect=Decision Maker reached and follow-up scheduled
- Renewal=any renewal date/annual product/service review period identified by contact other than decision maker (if applicable)
- Scheduled Call Back (Month)=contact other than decision maker requested call back
- Wrong Number=phone number reassigned

Yes, Mirror Appointment Setting has quite a few more than telemarketing would, but I strongly suggest you keep to these Status IDs and resist the urge to create more. I've come in to troubleshoot behind marketers who have created all sorts of Status IDs until they become meaningless. Sifting down to the most useful over 30 years of Mirror Appointment Setting has yielded this list – nothing more, nothing less.

In Mirror Appointment Setting, your progressive Status ID "Ladder" looks like this:

- Lead
- DM
- (optional) Renewal (if applicable)
- (optional) Scheduled Call Back
- Prospect
- Appointment

These are the Status IDs that matter for your Mirror Appointment Setting process. You can begin to think of yourself as a gardener and your CRM database as your garden. You need to keep your garden weed-free to help you along your way to growing long-term clients. All of the rest of the IDs are just to move or weed those contacts out of your regular call rotation, while keeping them organized. Let's get all of the other Status IDs out of the way, we'll then discuss your "Ladder" IDs in detail.

Dead

You've reached a contact who tells you they are no longer in business. This is the only reason to place a contact in this category. Resist the temptation to put contacts here for any other reason.

DNC

Decision makers specifically ask you to remove them from your list and Do Not Call them anymore. Please comply. Not only are we looking in the Mirror here and concluding we would want our wishes respected if this were us (and it likely has been!), but in Mirror Appointment Setting, we don't want to waste our time calling contacts who do not want to be called – period. End of story!

I've even coached decision makers who don't have the – well, whatever it is – assertiveness, perhaps – to just say "Please Do Not Call" or "Please Take Me Off Your List" who waste my time beating around the bush, trying to figure out how to tell me this is what they want. They usually let out a big sigh of relief because I gave them permission! I've even had some then want my "supervisor's" contact information so they can tell them how much they appreciated my "understanding." I tell them neither of us wants to waste our time – they are then in disbelief that I am acknowledging this and respecting their time. This is all due to the "slash and burn" telemarketing they've been subjected to. You are Mirror Marketers, make a difference by smiling and saying, "No Worries!" Then move on.

Disconnected

This seems obvious, but you'll encounter a lot of different recorded messages other than "this number is no longer in service." Here's the rule of thumb I use. If I get a recorded message that just says "this number has been disconnected" or "this number is no longer in service" I'm going to change this contact's Status ID to "Disconnected," and move on.

But what if you get a recording that says "all circuits are busy, please try your call again later," or "your call cannot be completed as dialed," but you double-checked that you dialed the number listed. These too could be disconnects, but I would leave them in your call rotation for a couple more rounds because they may just be temporary problems, and the next time you call, it could go through fine.

Other situations you may encounter that can be "precursors" to being on the way to a disconnected line is a fast tone – faster than a busy signal; no ring with just silence; or a ring, pick-up, then silence. I would leave all of these in your rotation for a few more rounds as well. I have seen it be just a temporary issue. You may also need to pay attention to the time you are calling. Some offices, especially Doctor's offices, disable their phones from ringing during lunch, so you will call and just find silence with no ring. Call after lunch and they are back to working fine.

Duplicate

Your CRM should have the ability to search and identify duplicate contacts, which is useful. You can then set one's Status

ID as duplicate to ensure you are not calling the same contact twice. Take the time to do this. Looking in the Mirror, imagine if you were called and you asked for a call back next week, only to be called back the next day. It is a quick way to alienate a prospect!

So do this, but realize that catching duplicates is going to be more complicated than running your CRMs duplicate search function, because it usually is simply searching for a matching phone number. There are a variety of ways for duplicates to go undetected by just searching for matching numbers. It would be great if companies and all of their divisions and iterations had the same name and number, but that is not real world.

Real world is that the same decision maker is responsible for several businesses. I call these "networked" contacts. When I run across one where I remember (and yes, recognizing something in common with two contacts is often the only way to catch duplicates) something in this contact that I saw in another contact, I'll first make a note that they may be a duplicate, and change their Status ID to "HOLD" until I can do a search to confirm they indeed are a duplicate.

For instance, this happens a lot with medical offices that I find out are owned by the local hospital, or schools that share a district business administrator as the decision maker. In fact, when I come across contacts that have a piece of information that suggests they are networked with another contact, I'll put them in HOLD right away, saving them for when I have a free moment to do some research and match them up.

Obviously, if the contact looks promising, I'll try to quickly do a search to link them up on the spot – but, remember, you are trying to keep your dials going, so be wise about whether to take the time or "HOLD" them to research later. Once designated as a duplicate, they are safely pulled out of your rotation.

Existing Client

Things happen. You may end of up with a contact in your list that is already a client. Just like in duplicate contacts, this can happen for a myriad of reasons – different phone number, different business name, one decision maker for several networked businesses. Quickly switch gears to, "Are we doing a good job?" You can turn what could be an embarrassing moment into a client satisfaction survey opportunity.

Remember to look in the Mirror – this is how you would want to be treated. Make sure you note their feedback, and if they need attention, make sure you pass that on to the appropriate people so they can be taken care of. Then just set their Status ID and move on.

Hold

Essentially, the "Hold" Status ID is to remove contacts from your regular rotation that are still potential prospects, but need more attention when you have time. In Mirror Appointment Setting, there is no "boiler room blitzing" going on, but you do want to keep your dials at a nice clip to get results. In addition, the contacts you designate as Holds need either more time or more attention before you call them again, or you could lose them altogether.

Your regular rotation is only for leads that you are rolling up the hill to being appointments. That is a big effort, so any leads that are an obstacle to achieving that smooth, constant line up the hill need to be placed out of the way for the time being. Think of calling your regular rotation as your prime-time activity. Any other activities need to wait for those times when it is less likely to reach decision makers.

Be careful with this Status ID, though. It is not a "catch-all." Only set the following contacts on Hold:

DM Hung Up

When a decision maker hangs up on you – don't take it personally. They are reacting to telemarketers. And even though as a Mirror Marketer, you will be able to reduce DM hang ups to a bare minimum, it still does occasionally happen. Just set them as a "Hold."

While you could call them back in a day or two, acknowledge they said they aren't interested right now, ask them if it is all right to contact them in the future, and when would be the best time if they agree (which they often do), this is not the best use of your prime-time, right?

You know they are a "no" now, but they could be a "yes" in the future. So it is better to set them as "Hold," to pull them out for special attention when you have time, so you don't leave a known "speed bump" in your prime-time regular rotation dials. It is also important from a mental perspective to keep "negatives" out of your regular rotation. Put them aside to work on at another time, so you can stay positive with unknown potentials and known prospects in your regular rotation.

DM will call if interested

You wonder when some decision makers like doctors and lawyers, who are tied to their clients by billable hours, can ever find time to make any decisions at all. I'm always amazed when I call a medical or professional office and the receptionist or office manager informs me that the professional is still the decision maker.

But it happens a lot. So, unless you're willing to go golfing with them, good luck with that! All kidding aside, send an email, then scuttle these professional decision makers to the "Hold" bin. You have to get back to your prime-time dials with potential decision-makers you actually have a chance of reaching.

When you have time, you can gather up these professional decision-makers out of your "Hold" cache for a marketing email campaign every so often throughout the year. You are still accomplishing your goal of making positive impressions on the off chance they may reach out to you, but you are then prioritizing your time in relationship to your potential results.

I am also seeing more and more decision makers working from home or at least off-site. Same response for the same reason: set them on "Hold" and include them in an occasional email campaign. When you call a contact a few times, and the receptionist tells you they don't have a set schedule, or they're "in and out" – off to "Hold" they go! I see this a lot with restaurants and retail, but it seems to be expanding across industries with the advent of telecommuting technology. Those that can are getting out of the office.

Seasonal

Obviously, you don't want to waste time dialing contacts when they're closed for the season. Set them to "Hold," and schedule a call back to pull them back into your regular dial rotation when they re-open. Then you'll just set their Status ID back to their previous ID (scan the notes) and begin calling them. If you don't get them to an appointment within their open season, do the same thing again, setting them to "Hold" until they re-open. Eventually, you'll either set an appointment with them or disqualify them.

Networked

You will encounter leads who are in a "network" structure with a number of variations. Common examples of networked leads are public schools, medical offices, hospitals, municipalities, but you will also find a wide variety of industries with a web that you have to follow to get to the decision maker. After all, entrepreneurs have been known to have their fingers in what seem like completely unrelated businesses and it's your job to track them down to set an appointment.

One stands out. He owned a conglomerate of websites, an ice cream shop and several B&Bs! I'm sure it made perfect sense to him—but it won't to you. It took some time to follow the thread, but he ended up making an appointment for them all.

The schools and hospitals follow a logical hierarchy, but don't expect all of the webs you need to follow to make any logical sense. Gathering the intel necessary to track down the decision maker can be tricky and time-consuming. With some networked leads, it's all about figuring out which hoops you have to jump through (and deciding if there's too many to make it worth your time). That's why you need to set them aside in "Hold". Think of them as puzzles to figure out when you get the chance.

Mail/Fax Only

Any contact request that requires you to get up from your seat, when you make your living being on the phone, needs to be set to "Hold." I run a paperless office by choice. When I encounter leads who expect me to fax or mail them information in this day and age (which is very rare), I interpret it as a brush-off by someone who doesn't know how to say "please do not call."

So, while I don't set them to "Dead" because I may decide to do a mail or fax campaign sometime for some reason, which they've given me permission to do (I'm a salesperson after all and hope really does spring eternal – a lead is never "dead" until they're really dead), I won't be sending them a paper letter or a fax any time soon. Just cheerfully set them to "Hold" so you can move on.

Not Qualified

Your company surely won't go on appointments with just anyone. They have some minimum qualifications that must be met for it to make sense for them to meet with an organization. It is your job as a Mirror Marketer to make sure, as soon as possible so you don't waste your time either, that every business is qualified.

It would be best if your company could qualify any businesses that make it onto your lead list prior to even putting them in your CRM to call. That would be the most efficient thing to do. But some qualifications are hard to determine ahead of time. Either way, you may encounter leads that are not qualified according to your company's required parameters, so you'll set them to "Not-Qualified."

Why do we not just set them to "Dead?" Because they are not dead – just not qualified at the present time. Things may change, and they may become qualified at some future date. I have also been contracted to call for several agents in the same company, and one agent's "not-qualified" is another agent's "qualified." So there is still viable business there, you just need to move the leads from where they are not qualified to where they are! More appointments for you.

Out of Area

Your company has a market area that they can reasonably cover through direct sales appointments. If you contact a lead and they state the decision maker is not in that market area, then you need to set them as "Out of Area."

Why do we not set them as "Dead?" Because they are not dead – just out of reach at the present time. While it is currently not feasible for your company's sales agent to go on an appointment with the decision maker, that may change in the future. Your company may broaden their market area to include the decision maker's location, and then you're back in the game with that lead.

Past Appointment

Why should you keep a past appointment cache? So many reasons! If the sales agent didn't close the deal on the first appointment, is there a window of opportunity for a second go? These are also your successes – the decision makers who said "yes." They could be important for strategic marketing analysis to see "what worked," they could be service surveys, they could provide you with statistics for making projections, they are established face-to-face relationships with your company that could be harvested in some yet-to-be-imagined way in the future.

Phone/Email Appointments

You keep your Phone/Email Appointment cache for the same reason as your Past Appointments. Your company may ask you to make the rounds again to see if there are any appointments to be had in this group. Realize, unless you have an Existing Client list provided to remove from this group, you may encounter existing clients, which you can simply turn into a client appreciation opportunity. You can also use the notes to do strategic marketing analysis on "what didn't work" as far as getting them to a face-to-face appointment, which could help you improve.

Wrong Number

Bet you're really wondering why we don't mark Wrong Numbers as Dead. Well – they're not dead – just reassigned. And what if they have been reassigned to a great new long-term client just waiting to be harvested? Again, it is a long shot because I see wrong numbers switching from business to residence as much as I see business to new business, but go ahead and put them aside for when you're willing to mine what might be there.

Now, we've dealt with all of the Status IDs that you need to prune out of your CRM regular rotation orchard. We can now focus on efficiently harvesting the fruit – those Status IDs that have the potential to yield appointments.

Status ID Ladder Game

Let's look at an overview of how our Status ID Ladder works. You can think of it as a strategic game if you want, where you have to achieve certain goals to advance to the next step. Yes, I'm totally playing a strategic game – with the thrill of the chase and the adrenaline rush of the win, and I encourage you to do the same!

My son constantly wanted me to play strategic games with him when I got home, and I kept begging for mindless games of luck instead, explaining I played strategic games with business development all day long, which I really enjoyed, but needed to rest my brain.

Thank God for role-playing card, video, and online games and lots of friends who liked to play them. We could never buy him video games and only rented them because he'd beat them in no time flat. He began creating games with rules of his own, once he'd mastered a game, to make it challenging again. Now that he has a career as a Sales Manager for the leading employee supplemental benefits company, he plays strategic games of his own all day (and is very good at it) – until he decides to retire early and create a real version of his own fantasy world.

My daughter is just as good at strategizing – but instead of playing games, she'd either go off to "observe" or just think (very logically I might add). Then, when the mood struck her, she'd enter a room, just take over as the natural leader, setting the agenda and rules of her own. She's about to step into her goal position of Offshore Internal Wholesaler for one of the top mutual fund companies – until she decides to go off the grid and live on a sailboat, or some other grand "my way" scheme. So they both now understand what I meant.

So let's play! Here we go with a general outline of the rules of our Status ID Ladder game: A "Lead" steps up to "DM" once the business has been qualified and the decision maker identified. A "DM" takes a step up to "Renewal" or "Scheduled Call Back" if you reach a particularly knowledgeable and helpful receptionist who knows enough to give you this information – the time when your company's product/service is on that contact's consideration radar. A "DM," or "Renewal," or "Scheduled Call Back," steps up to "Prospect" when you have successfully spoken to the decision maker, and you didn't yet set an appointment, but you formed an alliance with permission to provide future "service calls," until, hopefully one day, they agree to set an appointment. And last, a "Prospect" becomes an "Appointment" – SCORE! – when you've succeeded in setting an appointment!

Let's dig into each step on the ladder in more detail, so we can maximize your Mirror Marketer ability to win this game.

Lead

All businesses in your CRM start as Leads – or you can think of them as your seeds. They remain unplanted seeds until you can reach them and warm them up, starting them growing towards becoming an appointment. All Leads that you are unable to reach remain under this Status ID. In the beginning, this is all you have. As you begin to move contacts up the Status ID Ladder, this is the group that you will be calling during:

- Lunch (if contact is in a different time zone or you are working during lunch)
- Holidays (if you are working holidays)
- 4-5pm
- 9-9:30am

81

Why? Because your focus as Mirror Marketers with this group is to qualify and gather intel from receptionists only. But once you start moving contacts up the Status ID Ladder, you don't want to waste your time in the Leads when you can be reaching decision makers, so call Leads during the times when decision makers are least likely to be in. It's a complete waste of time to hear, "at lunch," or "not in yet," or "gone for the day," over and over, when it can totally be avoided.

One note here. Resist the temptation to throw any Leads into "Dead," even if it seems you are "unable" to reach them. "Leads" is where "unreachables" go. I can't tell you how many thousands (and I do mean thousands) of Leads I've dug out of the "Dead" Status ID group with just "busy," "n/a" (no answer), "gvm" (got voicemail), or "unable to reach," on them. "Dead" is only for "out of business." "Unable" to reach Leads are still seeds.

Don't get discouraged, keep trying – but only at the appropriate times. As you move contacts up the ladder, each Status ID has a different rhythm and flow. You'll come to appreciate the ebb and flow of Mirror Appointment Setting's different Status ID groups. The occasional ebb will give your brain a chance to refresh and regroup for your next strategic move in trying to win.

DM

Often, your leads will have a contact attached to it. Just about as often, this is not the decision maker for your company's product/service. If you assume it is, skip the qualifying/gathering intel call with the receptionist, and just ask for whomever is listed, you'll likely be wasting your time. Imagine that the contact is hard to reach. Since the president or CEO is usually the contact listed, they are very hard to reach or the receptionist is told to screen all of their calls.

You could just keep calling, never reach them and never know they are not the decision maker you need to speak to. You could also keep calling, if you didn't first qualify with the receptionist, finally reach the contact listed only to find out that the business is not qualified to even receive your calls (less than five employees, don't have benefits – whatever your company's qualifying requirements are that you could usually easily find out from the receptionist.)

If you do happen to get through to the president/CEO, you sound just like a telemarketer cold-calling, having made no effort to first learn about her business before wasting her time. Talk about chasing your tail. Your first call to a lead always needs to be your qualifying/intel call to the receptionist. You don't want to be asking for the wrong decision maker and you don't want to be wasting your time on a business not qualified for your company's product/service.

Once you have qualified and found out who the decision maker is from the receptionist, you can then change the contact, noting the information you are removing from the contact field for future reference (Notes: chngd DM Harry Bannock-President to Frank Conway-Controller) because you always want to gather additional intel, but never lose intel.

As you move through the lead list, gathering decision maker information and changing them to a "DM" Status ID, you'll soon have a batch of the "DMs" that can be searched and brought up to call at prime times. Congratulations! You're making your first step in our Mirror Status ID Ladder Game towards those appointment wins.

While you may occasionally get lucky and catch a decision maker in the "DM" Status ID group at just the right time to make an appointment, you are really after moving to one of the three next Status ID groups because that means you have found out when your decision maker is most likely to have your company's product/service on their radar for consideration.

I know, cold-callers/blitzers and what I've come to refer to as "slick willy" used car salesman types would say any time is the right time to shove through a sale or appointment. But in Mirror Appointment Setting, we are treating our potential clients the way we would want to be treated, we are being patient, creating an alliance and going with their flow.

So, as a Mirror Marketer, your ultimate goal, short of asking for an appointment, is to receive permission for future "service calls." If you reach the decision maker and they tell you they just renewed their current version of your product/service, your answer is: "No worries! Is it all right if we touch base with you next year?" Literally, nine times out of ten, you can feel their defenses melt away, and a whole new refreshing dynamic fills the phone line, as they reply, with surprise, "Sure!" In this moment, you have just made a full transition from interruption to ally – to support team -- for your new prospect.

Let's focus on the three remaining Status IDs in our Ladder Game that allow you to actually schedule a follow-up.

Renewal

A lot of products/services have an annual renewal or review time. Obviously, if you can find out when that time is, from either the receptionist (preferable) or the decision maker, you once again are turning what used to be an interruption into a valuable service. Looking in the Mirror, imagine you are that decision maker and making decisions about a particular product/service is just one thing you have on your plate. Then you receive a call from a polite, professional Mirror Marketer at just the right time to set up an appointment to gather information or a quote on that product/service. Talk about feeling you are being catered to! That's the "magic" of Mirror Appointment Setting.

Once you find out the renewal/review time, and set the Status ID, you can then schedule your "service call" at just the right time. I often schedule four months ahead of the actual renewal/review time. That way I can first send a couple email reminders to let the decision maker know I'll be contacting them. These emails are also part of your service, to remind them this decision time is heading their way.

Scheduled Call Back

You're not always able to obtain the renewal/review time, but often, the receptionist will suggest a call back time (and you should always ask.) You can still advance to the next step in our Status ID Ladder Game with this information. Set the Status ID for the month suggested, and then schedule your follow up call. This at least gets you warmer in regards to the best time to call the decision maker regarding your company's product/service. Receptionists' heads are packed with information sometimes they don't even realize they know.

If you were to ask them why you should call then, just out of curiosity, they may not be able to pinpoint why, or you could hear a myriad of answers from "we'll have our year-end finished," or "that's our slow season," or just "it seems like that's about when (the decision maker) makes a lot of those types of decisions." As long as you've built rapport and made the receptionist feel appreciated, never discount any piece of intel -- inside information – they give you. Be grateful, grateful, grateful – which is at the foundation of being a Mirror Marketer.

Prospect

Congratulations! You reached a decision maker, and while they did not agree to an appointment today, they did agree to some type of follow-up, whether it is next week or next year! When you speak to a decision maker, and receive permission to move forward, even if it is at some seemingly far off future date, you can now set your Status ID to Prospect. You are now just one step away from winning our Status ID Ladder Game – one step away from setting an appointment!

The goal of our game is to gradually move as many of your leads to prospects with scheduled follow-ups as you can. You may have heard of a "sales pipeline." Here is Mirror Appointment Setting's version. You constantly keep moving prospects into our "appointment pipeline" that flows all year round, providing you with a constant, steady source of appointments. We'll go into great detail about your process schedule coming up, but just imagine opening up your CRM each day to find a follow-up Task List of prospects that you scheduled last week or last month popping up for you to call. Imagine each month finding a slew of prospects to call that you scheduled last year. This is what it's all about. This is the heart of Mirror Appointment Setting and being a true Mirror Marketer. When you put in the effort each moment each day with each person you speak to, your CRM garden begins to bloom, your CRM orchard begins to bear fruit.

Now the cold-call/blitz/slick willy proponents might say you'll starve till then. Interestingly enough – you don't. As I've stated, I've done it all, and over 30+ years, my Mirror approach has always yielded more appointments by a significant "how did you do that" margin. Why? I have to believe it is because it is founded on the Golden Rule – simply treating others the way you want to be treated. No fear, no desperation – just respect. Maybe it really is receiving what you send – what goes around comes around. You can feel really good as a Mirror Marketer about what you do.

Appointment

You did it! You made an appointment and won the game! Click on the Status ID and set it to "Appointment" with pride. You set a qualified appointment with the decision maker in the sales schedule provided to you by your company. Schedule the appointment, as well as a confirmation call two days prior, email an appointment confirmation to the prospective client, and email the appointment contact report to the appropriate person. Your company may have designated a sales coordinator, sales manager or the sales agent themselves.

A note about setting "tentative" appointments. Be careful. It's a slippery slope. Personally, if I have a decision maker who is waffling about a solid time, I pull back. If they really want to set an appointment, they always pull me back in to set a solid date and time. And even then, I'm still allowing them an out by saying, "you're sure." Some would say it is using reverse psychology. I would say I'm just looking in the Mirror, and giving them some air, which is what I would want if it were me. I want it to be their decision, I want them to own it, or I let them know I'm willing to totally back away.

Occasionally, you'll encounter a decision maker who does this waffling to play an ego game. They derive a feeling of power in playing what I call the "stroke me" game. I refuse to play. Let go, tell them they can call you if they're interested and move on. Honestly, I'm unable to take this person serious as a professional – grow up already! There are enough professional, respectful business people to do business with – if this decision maker wants to play this game with you, they'll likely play it with your sales agent, too, which is an utter waste of everyone's time. You not only need to respect others, you need to respect yourself. Have a healthy self respect. Let go. As I do that Mirror self-reflection thing, I conclude that letting go in appointment setting, in sales, business and life in general, turns out to be very powerful. It is not possible in a cold call/blitz/slick willy approach, which are all fear-based. Letting go is fearless. And when fear is not present, your cup can be filled up with other great things like confidence, respect – even love – and you will prosper.

Tracking Your Results

Your company will be able to run reports from your CRM to help them and you track your progress as a Mirror Marketer. If you faithfully play our Status ID Ladder Game, you'll be able to pinpoint your strengths and areas where you have room to grow. You will also be able to separate out what you can control – and what you can't. You can't control the quality of the lead list. That is up to your company. Unfortunately, it doesn't matter how much companies have paid for lists and how many promises they've been made about the quality of those lists – every list I've ever called falls short.

Honestly, the phone book may be better and newer information than any expensive, hyped-up list I've called. Don't know what is so hard about "scrubbing" lists – you just call and verify information with receptionists and other sources in a constant rotation. I end up "scrubbing" every list I call myself because it hasn't been done and I'd rather look like a fool with a receptionist rather than a decision maker – even though that still is not good, and companies ought to be able to get what they've been promised. Is it a complete waste of time? Totally – that is not our job. But if it hasn't been done, we end up doing it.

Imagine what we could accomplish if all of the weeding was already done, and we could just focus on the Status ID Ladder Game! It is an area where your company can focus to make your efforts more efficient, and significantly increase your results.

The information provided in your CRM Reports gives your company the ability to hold their list provider accountable – and it allows you both to hold YOU accountable only for the results you can control. Using the CRM Report, you can track your daily ratios. It's fun to watch your improvement over time. I enjoy tracking and I suppose I make a game out of it, too. Set personal goals and see if you can achieve them. When you've achieved them, set some more – never stop playing the self-improvement game!

So what's next? Well, we've covered your set-up from your email signature to your phone scripts to setting up your CRM. It's time to put it all into action!

A Day in the Life of a Mirror Marketer

You're all set-up – now it's time to put all the pieces into play and dial. I really do like to play – so that's what we're going to do here. We're going to role-play. I'm going to write the *Day in the Life of a Mirror Marketer* screenplay, hoping this format will not only help you visualize yourself playing the Mirror Marketer role, but help you catch all of the nuances that can make a significant difference in reaching your ultimate heights of success. Ready?

INT. YOUR COMPANY, YOUR MIRROR MARKETER STATION, 9AM

A well-lit, comfortable quiet space.

A zero gravity chair, a computer screen projected onto the ceiling, a wireless keyboard, mouse, and headset. A side table with a phone, a paper calendar lined out on a steno pad, a mug warmer with a mug of hot mint tea, and a coaster with a large bottle of water on it.

MIRROR MARKETER (MM) climbs into the chair, and lays it back to zero gravity position. Comfortable, your focus turns to the computer screen on the ceiling. The desktop has three folders and two documents in a row.

> ➢ Folder 1 – Appointments
> ➢ Folder 2 – Backups
> ➢ Folder 3 – Contact Reports
> ➢ Document 1 – Phone Script
> ➢ Document 2 – Marketing Email

You open the Contact Report folder, and see a month's worth of Contact Report Forms. You click on today's date to open your Daily Contact Report to be filled in today as you call.

You then open your CRM software, position it to the right of your screen, and click on today's Follow-Ups. A list of contacts appears before you. You do a Status ID sort to group your follow-up IDs together to be called in order of priority:

➢ Appointments to confirm.

➢ Prospects whom agreed to a follow-up call.

➢ DMs to whom you've sent an introduction marketing email, and they now need an intro follow-up call.

You then open the Phone Script document and position it beside your CRM on the left side of your screen.

You then open the Marketing Email document, highlight the entire email and copy it, ready to paste into emails.

You glance at your paper calendar, orienting yourself to which dates you'll be calling for today. You look at next week and the week after – those are your target dates to schedule appointments for today.

Looking at your CRM, since this is your first day, you don't yet have any Appointments, Prospects or DMs to call, so you perform a search for Leads. All of your contacts in your brand new list are Leads. You see each contact has the name of the company, a contact name, title, phone, address, number of employees and type of business.

The first business in the list is Advanced Roofing, you see Al Moyer is listed as the contact, and that 10 is listed as the number of employees.

You dial the number. And begin a note with your initials.

RECEPTIONIST:

"Advanced Roofing, this is Kathy, how may I help you?"

MM:

(Cheerful) *"Hi Kathy. I hope you can. This is (You) over at (Sales Agent's Name) office. I was first, trying to reach your (product/service) person, and second, so I don't waste their time, I need to verify (qualifier), if you knew."*

RECEPTIONIST:

"Well, I wouldn't know – but Diane handles that. Hold on."

MM:

"Thanks, Kathy."

You type "Diane is DM" in the note and wait, then receive Diane's voicemail.

DIANE (voicemail message)

"Hi. This is Diane. I'm either on the phone or away from my desk. Please leave a message."

You hang up. Then you type "gvm" for "got voicemail" in the note. You did identify the decision maker, so you set the Status ID to "DM," which signals the CRM to begin a "DM" group, moving this contact out of the "Lead" list.

You move on to the next contact. It is Advanced Medical, Barry Golis MD is the contact name, and 20 is the employee number.

RECEPTIONIST:

"Doctor's office, how may I direct your call."

MM:

"Hi, I'm hoping you can help me. This is (You) over at (Sales Agent's Name) office. I'm first, trying to reach your (product/service) person, and second, so I don't waste their time, I'm hoping to verify (qualifier), if you knew."

RECEPTIONIST:

"Let me get you to the Office Manager. Hold on."

MM:

"Thanks."

SUE:

"This is Sue. May I help you?"

MM:

(Professional – Confident) *"Hi Sue. I'm hoping you can. This is (You) over at (sales agent's name) office, and I was first trying to reach (product/service) person, and second, so I don't waste their time, I was hoping to verify (qualifier), if you knew."*

SUE:

"The doctor makes those decisions. Mail some information, and he'll call you if he's interested."

MM:

(Matter of fact) *"We actually went paperless, is there an email I could send him information to?"*

SUE:

"We don't give out emails. Sorry."

MM:

"Thanks for your time."

You make a note that looks like this: "(Your Initials) rec. > Office Mgr – Sue – Dr is DM, can't give email, mail only." You then make a new note: "Hold – mail only." You then set the Status ID to "Hold."

Next contact, Advantage Security, contact name is Sandra Andrews-CEO, employee number is 100. You dial.

(RECORDED GREETING):

"Thank you for calling Advantage Security. If you know your party's three digit extension, you can dial it at any time..."

You press "O".

RECEPTIONIST:

"Advantage Security. This is Lorraine. How may I help you?"

MM:

(Inquisitive) *"Hi. I'm hoping you can. This is (You) over at (sales agent's name) office, and I was first trying to reach (product/service) person, and second, so I don't waste their time, I was hoping to verify (qualifier), if you knew."*

RECEPTIONIST:

"We (qualifier) in May and Sandra handles that, but she's not in yet today, I can put you into her voicemail."

MM:

"Actually, would you happen to have an email for her? Then I can just send this over."

RECEPTIONIST:

"Sure. It's sandrews AT advantagesecurity DOT com."

MM:

"Thanks so much, Lorraine."

You make a note: "(Your Initials) (Qualifier) is May, Sandra is DM, email is *sandrews AT advantagesecurity DOT com* per Lorraine." You then send Sandra your marketing email, make a new note: (Your Initials) sent Sandra info email." You also notate an email sent on your Contact Report.

Next contact, QuickRite Plumbing & Heating, contact name is Russell Sanders-owner, employee number is 5. You dial.

RUSSELL:

"Hello?"

MM:

"Hi. Is this QuickRite Plumbing & Heating? Is this Russell?"

RUSSELL:

"Yes. Who's this?"

MM:

(Upbeat & Casual) *"Hi Russell. This is (You) over at (sales agent's name), (your company). (sales agent's name) asked me to give you a call. We weren't sure (qualifier). (sales agent's name) was hoping to provide you with a (product/service) comparison to see if we're a fit, if you were open to that."*

RUSSELL:

"Not interested" (Hangs Up).

You make a note: (Your Initials) "Russell ni (for "not interested") hung-up." Then make a new note: (Your initials) Hold-DM ni hung-up" and set the Status ID to "Hold."

Next contact, Daylight Salon & Spa, contact name is Angel Sanchez-owner, employee number is 20. You dial.

RECEPTIONIST:

"Thank you for calling Daylight Salon & Spa. This is Tiffany, how may I help you?"

MM:

(Inquisitive & Friendly) *"Hi Tiffany. I'm hoping you can. This is (You) over at (sales agent's name) office, and I was first trying to reach (product/service) person, and second, so I don't waste their time, I was hoping to verify (qualifier), if you knew."*

RECEPTIONIST:

"Angel is right here, hold on."

You make a note: "Angel-..."

ANGEL:

"This is Angel."

MM:

(Confident & Casual) *"Hi Angel. This is (You) over at (sales agent's name), (your company). (sales agent's name) asked me to give you a call. We weren't sure (qualifier). (sales agent's name) was hoping to provide you with a (product/service) comparison to see if we're a fit, if you were open to that."*

ANGEL:

"I just met with my current (product/service) rep, and she said the prices are all the same."

MM:

(Attentive) *"You would think that would be the case, but I just spoke to an electrical contractor who had stayed with the same (product/service) agent for 25 years. Then his son joined the business and convinced him to check with other agents, and he ended up saving $8,300 a year for the same exact (product/service) – just a different agent. I was amazed!"*

ANGEL:

"Really. Hmm..."

MM:

(Light and easy going) *"Of course, who knows if that would be your experience, but I could have (sales agent's name) stop by next Tuesday, the 15ᵗʰ at 10am if that would work for you, just to see if we can provide you with a better value."*

ANGEL:

"Next Tuesday at 10? Afternoon would work better."

MM:

"How would 2pm be?"

ANGEL:

"That would work. What's your name and number just in case."

You type while talking: "Angel – set appt Tuesday, (month) 15, (year) at 2pm."

MM:

(Professional "all taken care of" tone) *"I'll email you a confirmation that will have all of our information, then I'll call a couple days ahead just to remind you. What is your email address?"*

ANGEL:

"That would be great. It's angel AT daylightspa DOT com."

You type email address.

MM:

"I just need to verify a few things for (sales agent's name). Could you verify your address for me?

ANGEL:

"5001 Broadway, Suite 200"

You type "verified address."

MM:

"Great! That's what we have. How many (qualifiers) do you currently have?"

ANGEL:

"5."

You type: "# of (qualifier) 5."

MM:

"And your current (product/service) company?

ANGEL:

"(Current company.)"

You type: "current (company name)."

MM:

(Grateful & Enthusiastic) *"Great! We're all set. (sales agent's name) will be there next Tuesday, the 15th at 2pm. I hope we're a fit!"*

ANGEL:

"Thank you. Goodbye."

You then schedule the appointment, send an email confirmation (using your email template) to Angel. You scan the CRM fields making sure all of the information is correct, then create a Daylight Salon & Spa Contact Report, send (coordinator/manager/sales agent) a new appointment email (using your email template) with the contact report attached. You then set the Status ID to "Appointment."

Next contact, Loud Media, contact name is Julie Goodwin-President, employee number is 50. You dial.

(RECORDED GREETING):

"Thank you for calling Loud Media. Please listen as our menu has recently changed. For Sales..."

You hit "0," and the greeting starts over, so you wait.

(RECORDED GREETING):

"Thank you for calling Loud Media. Please listen as our menu has recently changed. For Sales, press 1, for Julie, press 2, for George, press 3, for Nubia, press 4, for Sanjeet press 5, for the operator press 9, or stay on the line."

You press 9.

RECEPTIONIST:

"Loud Media. This is Megan, how may I help you?"

MM:

(Professional & Confident) *"Hi Megan. I'm hoping you can. This is (You) over at (sales agent's name) office, and I was first trying to reach (product/service) person, and second, so I don't waste their time, I was hoping to verify (qualifier), if you knew."*

MEGAN:

"We're not interested."

MM:

(Cheerful) *"No worries. Is it all right if we touch base next year?"*

MEGAN:

"That's fine."

MM:

"When would be the best time to call (or qualifier)?

MEGAN:

"We don't take a look at that until next fall."

MM:

"Great. I'll touch back then. Who should I ask for?"

MEGAN:

"Nubia or George."

MM:

(Sincere) *"Thanks so much, Megan."*

You make a note: "(Your initials) spoke to Megan; ni; touchbase reb. (for rebuttal); review next fall; Nubia or George DMs; cb." Then schedule a follow-up – they review in fall, so September, but set for August to leave pre-follow up email reminder time. Make a new note: "(Your initials) chngd DM Julie Goodwin-President to Nubia" (since she said her name first). Then change Status ID to "CB Aug."

Next contact, Tropical Syrup Mfg, contact name is Wheeler Godfrey-President, employee number is 100. You dial.

(RECORDED ON HOLD MESSAGE) Latin music playing with narrator:

"Tropical syrup is all natural with no artificial colors, flavors and no preservatives. It's perfect for mixing with…"

RECEPTIONIST:

"Tropical Syrup, may I help you?"

MM:

"Hi. I'm hoping you can. This is (You) over at (sales agent's name) office, and I was first trying to reach (product/service) person, and second, so I don't waste their time, I was hoping to verify (qualifier), if you knew."

RECEPTIONIST:

"Please hold."

WHEELER:

"Wheeler."

MM:

"Hi Wheeler. This is (You) over at (sales agent's name), (your company). (sales agent's name) asked me to give you a call. We weren't sure (qualifier). (sales agent's name) was hoping to provide you with a (product/service) comparison to see if we're a fit, if you were open to that."

WHEELER:

"Well, Joe would really handle that. He'll gather the information, then we'll discuss it. Let me transfer you to him."

MM:

"Thank you."

JOE:

"Joe Frintino."

MM:

"Hi Joe. I just spoke to Wheeler and he said I should speak to you. This is (You) over at (sales agent's name), (your company). (sales agent's name) asked me to give you a call. We weren't sure (qualifier). Wheeler said (sales agent's name) needs to schedule with you to do a (product/service) comparison. Would next Wednesday, the 16th at 10am work for you?"

JOE:

"I'm out at a conference all next week, and don't yet know my schedule after that. Could you call me in a couple weeks?"

MM:

"Sure. Talk to you then."

You make a note: "(Your initials) Wheeler – final DM, Joe – 1st point DM, cb two weeks." Then you schedule a call back for two weeks, and set the Status ID to "Prospect."

You continue to call, making 15-20 dials an hour, interspersed with sending emails and making notes. And, at the end of your eight hour day, (taking time for lunch and bathroom breaks, of course) you've made 120-160 dials, and sent several marketing emails. You're ready to wrap it up for your first day. Your Daily Contact Report has the emails filled in that you entered throughout the day. Now it's time to do a CRM Daily Contact Activity report to complete it. You run the report, and record the "Discard" Status ID #s – Disconnects, Not Qualified, etc.; the "Process" Status ID #s – Leads, Holds, DMs, and CBs; the Prospects - listing company, contact and call back date; and your Appointment - listing company, contact and date/time. You send your Daily Contact Report and call it a day!

~~**~~

Was that helpful? Did you have fun stepping into the Mirror Marketer role? I hope so. There are unlimited scenario variations, but I tried to cover the more common ones. Of course, I didn't go over the "Discard" contact scenarios. How many of those you face depend entirely upon how fresh and accurate the lead list is that your company has provided.

Our *Day in the Life of a Mirror Marketer* screenplay exercise not only paints a picture of what to say, but more importantly, how to say it. You may have heard the adage, "It's not what you say, it's how you say it." There is truth in that. If each receptionist and each decision maker you speak to hears you speaking the way you would like to be spoken to, just imagine what you can accomplish!

So this plays out your first day as a Mirror Marketer, what's next? As you chomp through your CRM like pacman/pacwoman, dialing the leads, and weeding them out or moving them up the Status ID Ladder, you'll begin to have several groups of contacts that you'll be rotating in an ongoing schedule. We can now layer a new level on top of our basic Status ID Ladder Game. In order to keep moving contacts up our Ladder, your overriding goal (looking in the Mirror) is to not tick anyone off, so you can keep calling them!

Scheduling

I'm amazed when I troubleshoot and come into a situation where the marketer training says to call a decision maker daily, completely ignoring the fact that there is, 9 times out of 10, a receptionist involved. What do you think is going to happen if you call a receptionist every day? Click -- or "YOU JUST CALLED YESTERDAY! I PASSED ON YOUR MESSAGE! IF WE'RE INTERESTED WE'LL CALL! STOP CALLING!" I can just hear this receptionist ranting to the decision maker about you – and your company after they slam down the phone. What do you think your chances are then? Zero. It's such a common sense thing. Just look in the Mirror. How would you feel if you were this receptionist?

Even if that 1 time out of 10, you've managed to obtain the decision maker's direct extension, don't wear it out! Most everyone these days has caller id, so the decision maker you are trying to reach can see your bajillion calls -- tread lightly.

Or, how about when you've sent an introduction email, left a follow-up voicemail, then you keep calling and the decision maker keeps telling the receptionist they are "unavailable" when you call. Unless you have more information, you have likely run into the type of decision maker who will never take your call. Now, it is true, for whatever reason, they don't tell the receptionist to tell you they are not interested at this time, which is just as easy and would seem to make more sense than "unavailable."

It almost makes you think they like being chased. Complete waste of time. Again, I don't have time for power games -- I refuse to play. You've built rapport with the receptionist who is caught in the middle, right? Try to figure out if this is a power game or if the decision maker warrants another call, and is truly unavailable right now, by asking the receptionist "what is the best time to call?" Pay careful attention to the receptionist's answer. If you're reaching the "hounding" line, they'll let you know. They are usually very aware if a decision maker likes to play power games because they are always caught in the middle, not that some receptionists don't like to play power games with you, too – disengage and move on.

This goes for emails as well. Remember, you are trying to form an alliance, turning contacts into prospects until they are ready to become clients. Respect their wishes. Look in the Mirror, and imagine yourself in the decision maker's position. How many marketing emails do you imagine they receive per day? While they may have great spam filters, how many other, legitimate business emails are they receiving daily to manage? Lots! If you were in their position, how many emails how often would you consider to be helpful as reminders, and hopefully resources, without crossing over to hounding?

What is the definition of "hounding"? Well, look in the mirror, and imagine yourself running through a forest being chased by loud hound dogs hot on your trail. How do you feel about those hound dogs? Don't be a hound dog making your potential prospect feel like your prey. You and your company's product/service are, instead, a patient suitor waiting respectfully for the opportunity to create a long-term client relationship with your prospect.

With all of this in mind, let me set down the general guidelines that serve me well.

General Mirror Scheduling Guidelines

In general, once I initiate an introduction email and call with a decision maker, I schedule them for a call and make sure to leave a message or voicemail (preferable) before I put them back into the unscheduled "DM" group, to be called in my regular rotation. For scheduled follow-ups, I set them up on a regular call schedule attempting to reach them over the course of usually a month. Several factors come into play to determine exactly how their specific call schedule will transpire. The business type and size is one factor. The receptionist's approach is another. The decision maker's contact system is yet another.

Managing Business Types & Sizes

Sizes:

Less than 5 employees – The decision maker may answer the phone! Be ready! How do you know if it is the decision maker you have on the phone? Hmmm... I can usually tell. But I have to think about why I know that in order to tell you. Without just saying, "I have a feeling," I would have to say their tone sounds busy – but confident. A receptionist can answer and sound busy, but, yes, there is a confidence in a decision maker's tone a receptionist just doesn't have. I told you about the nuances! They really matter! Listen for it.

If you think you have a decision maker on the phone, go ahead and ask "is this (decision maker's name)?" Now, sometimes, they don't want to admit it. So they'll say "who's calling?" They'll try to qualify you before they admit their identity. You just need to be straightforward with them, and respectfully answer. Honestly, when a decision maker is always answering their own phone, look in the Mirror, and realize they are getting your call and everyone else's, so you face a higher level of "not interested" and hang ups. Don't take it personal. It is a reaction to telemarketers who are not as respectful as you are as a Mirror Marketer. If you can, squeeze in *"No worries! Is it all right if we touch base in the future (or if your product/service is on a cycle, then "next year" or __) just to make sure you're still okay,"* you'll usually get a refreshing response – and you've succeeded in jumping from step "Lead" in our Status ID Ladder Game all the way up to "Prospect" in one call! If a receptionist answers the phone, they may be the decision maker's spouse – treat them as a co-decision maker. If not the spouse, the receptionist will wear many hats – so, on the plus side, they may have a great deal of knowledge and can be very helpful.

5-9 employees – You may encounter the same scenario as less than five employees. Or, I've noticed, with this size company, the owner is often out on jobs or on the road selling. You may encounter an office manager as decision maker, which is good, or an owner who is trying to do it all, retaining all decision making, in addition to going on jobs or doing the majority of the selling, which is not so good. If you encounter an "in and out" or never available owner/decision-maker, after your initial introduction email and message (they don't usually have voicemail), you may have to set this contact's Status ID as "Hold" – "DM will call if int," and possibly set them up on an occasional email campaign to continue layering your positive impressions.

10-19 employees – You may start to see some more task specialization – possibly a person tasked with HR, and a bookkeeper. The owner may still be heading up marketing and sales. Structure starts to vary more with the type of business. There is more likely to be a receptionist and an office manager. The receptionist may try to hand you off to the office manager, even though the owner is still likely the final decision maker.

20-50 employees – Depending on what your product/service is and who is likely to be your decision maker, you may start to encounter controllers, finance directors at this level who are tasked with purchasing and HR directors tasked with any personnel-related purchases. In reality, the owner/president/CEO is likely still pretty hands-on in final decision making, and the specialists are information gatherers.

50-99 employees – At this level, in general, you can start to see the controllers, finance directors, HR directors beginning to make final decisions. Or, a two level decision process, where your sales agent will need to meet with the specialist, then either the specialist will present to the final decision makers in a separate meeting or will have the "short-listed" sales agent come back for a second meeting with the "brass."

100-499 employees – Specialists usually are the final decision makers at this level, with President/CEO being apprised of the choice, and just signing off on it unless they see a huge red flag. You also are more likely to have fun with the greeting loop and employee directory – but on the bright side, it may be easier to get your decision maker's direct extension using the staff directory, which has obvious advantages. If I'm not ever able to reach the decision maker on their direct extension, though, I'll often go back to the receptionist trying to get "best-time-to-call" information to increase my chances.

500-999 employees – At this level, you may encounter a phone system with a greeting loop that only allows department or staff extensions or you'll reach a receptionist who is really just an operator routing calls and is all too happy to say, "I don't know, I'm just the operator." Choosing the department from the directory that is the best likely match for your company's product/service may be your best bet here. Then use your receptionist qualifying script with the person who answers.

At this level, you might also start to hear that the decisions are made elsewhere. Depending on how your company manages their sales territory, this may be an "out of area" situation. Clarify where the decisions are made, if it is still within your company's marketing territory, try to get the phone number and decision maker's name, update that information in your CRM – and keep climbing!

If decisions are made in-house, you'll likely start to encounter assistants to the decision makers that are screening, but not always. Assistants can provide a wealth of information, especially regarding the decision maker's process and schedule -- it doesn't mean you're done. Remember, you are also an assistant – build rapport, ask for their help. Continue to seek an audience with the decision maker. With positive email and message impressions, the decision maker could very well tell the assistant to set up a meeting on their schedule. At the very least, if the decision maker tells the assistant to tell you they are not interested, it is usually "at this time," which leaves you a window to form an alliance of "service calls" in the future.

1000+ employees - Same phone system challenges as 500 – 999 employees. Same potential for "out of area" – often a bit more of a chance for out of state or even out of country decision making. These companies are often – but not always – thickly networked with a long, complicated decision-making process. As with any of the levels, there are always exceptions. These companies tend to take longer and need more intel gathering to weave your way to the actual final decision maker for your company's product/service. But, of course, given their size, it is often well worth the effort.

Just don't lose sight of the forest for this one tree. It may end up that they may require a specific proposal process and have specific guidelines to follow, which then needs to be turned over to sales staff. You still need to accomplish your daily dials, rather than risk too much time on one company. It is still a numbers game. You may have to put these companies in "Hold," as "networked," and tend to them every so often when you are ahead in your dials to keep climbing.

Once you have gathered the decision maker and process intel, you can turn it over. Then, even if you didn't make an appointment, try to track the sales team's progress with this company – if they win, know that you have also won. You started the ball rolling. Place the results in that contact's notes in your CRM, and mark it somehow, so that when it is Performance Review time, you can run a report of these results that don't show up in the appointment statistics to toot your own horn. Use this information to ask for a raise, a preferred schedule or ?!

Types:

There are some generalities that can be made regarding business types that may help you navigate – but never forget there are always exceptions, and you have to constantly be perceptive, able to "think on the phone" to maximize your success as a Mirror Marketer. Sound hard? It really isn't. All you really need to do is look in the Mirror and LISTEN.

Professional Offices: There is usually a receptionist and an office manager. If the principals are still making decisions, rather than turning them over to the office manager, it is very difficult, if not impossible, to reach the principal. They only make money for billable client hours so they are literally tied to their clients and during working hours they are "unavailable." Doctors, Dentists, Veterinarians, Lawyers, CPAs, Investment Advisors, Insurance and Real Estate are examples.

You'll also often find that if the principals are men, the principals' wives are the decision makers (doctors & dentists especially), and are working from home. Don't give up, though! Professional Offices need products/services, too. Accept that you may have to set these contacts at "Hold" Status IDs, with "DM will call if interested," but you can continue to make positive impressions. Set them up for a quarterly email campaign, hopefully sending them useful resources regarding your product/service.

I have actually received calls from office managers who have been told by principals to set an appointment. It is rare, but it does happen. Also realize they may be contacting your sales agent directly as a result of your email marketing campaigns. It would be great if you could track these. Every positive impression layer does count.

Trades: Unless trades have elevated to the level of manufacturing, these types of businesses are hit and miss as to whether you can reach the decision maker. Sometimes, the owner has turned over decision making to an office manager, who is often also the receptionist, wearing many hats, which is great. More often, they have not, and you'll hear they're "in and out" a lot. The owner is often the plumber, electrician, construction foreman and they are out on jobs. Ask the receptionist/office manager the best time to call, and you may be able to determine a time to call when the decision maker is most likely to be at the office.

You may want to try for a month, then schedule another email/call campaign next quarter. Keep stacking those positive impressions layers – just keep the receptionist/office manager in mind, and what you believe would accomplish your goal without annoying them.

You will also tend to see trades trying to avoid face-to-face appointments and wanting to receive email prices. This is because either the decision maker is so hard to pin down for a meeting or, if the receptionist/office manager is the decision maker, they are often wearing so many hats, it's hard to breathe. I understand, but I actually started pointing out they could get impersonal prices online, but personal, customized quotes require a face-to-face meeting. Form an alliance, be an ally. (Respectful) persistence pays off.

Retail: Retail can be unpredictable. With some stores, the owner practically lives there, and seems to be running it solo – could be an easy appointment. Yet, even with a very small retail business, it may also be hard to catch the decision maker in. Right away, try to determine if the decision maker has a set schedule when they're at the store. It's often hit and miss. Some decision makers work from home, or they have more than one location and bounce around. You'll find staff who answer the phone don't often know much. Try to call at the best time for a month, then set up a quarterly email/call campaign. The nice thing about when you do reach the decision maker, if they need your product/service, it will often be a quick decision to make an appointment, as their schedule is often more predictable than some of the other businesses.

Restaurants: Restaurants are similar to retail. In addition, staff who answer the phone are usually very busy, they rarely know the decision maker's email or other information. Ask for the manager on duty. They often still do not have an email address for the decision maker. You may be able to avoid the "very busy" challenge by making sure you're not calling a restaurant at meal times – breakfast, lunch, dinner. If you are unable to obtain an email for the owner/decision maker, just schedule them for a quarterly phone campaign. That's the best you can do.

Manufacturing: You would think manufacturers would be large companies, but there are many smaller manufacturers. You'll see the employee size, with the above guidelines applying, from even 10 employees and up. The employee size guidelines are more applicable than any specifics regarding type, per se.

Unless they are very small, you will often encounter a controller/HR director who is either the decision maker or on the decision making team. A few times, with small to medium manufacturers, I have actually been transferred right to the President/CEO, who then refers me to the controller/HR director. Easy appointment. Perhaps they don't have as many demands on their time, overseeing a "well-oiled manufacturing machine"?

Schools: I consider schools as "network" contacts and usually set them as "Hold" Status IDs, to be worked on when I've managed to get ahead in my dials. The structure is usually all schools linking to a superintendent's office and a business administrator is the decision maker – but not really, because they have to submit most decisions to the school board. It can get quite convoluted.

I've also found schools can be members of associations for products/services. It's not that they will not look at anything else, it just makes it a bit harder. The association is "comfortable" and all of the other schools are in it. Keep trying – just don't spend oodles of time. An exception with schools is pre-schools, which are often private and have one decision maker who is fairly easy to track down. If your product/service is a fit, a pre-school often is an easy appointment.

Hospitals: I've encountered a lot of hospitals buying up lots of medical clinics, doctor's offices and medical-related businesses. I gather them all in a "Hold" Status IDs as "network" contacts. It's quite a maze to unravel. They often also require an RFP (Request For Proposal) and have a long decision making process. Gather what intel you can, then it is likely a turn to the sales team. Like with the 1000+ employees companies, even if you didn't make an appointment, try to track the sales team's progress with this hospital – if they win, know that you have also won. You started the ball rolling. Place the results in that contact's notes in your CRM, and mark it somehow, so that when it is Performance Review time, you can run a report of these results that don't show up in the appointment statistics to toot your own horn.

Municipalities: You'll encounter the odd sewer authority, water company, mechanic shop and others that end up being part of a municipality. Gather them up and put them all on a "Hold" Status ID as "network" contacts. If you want to pursue more intel, you'll need to contact the municipality and will likely be directed to the purchasing agent who then tells you they have an annual purchasing process, and that they "take bids" via RFPs. Again, like the hospitals and the 1000+ employee companies, once you gather as much intel as possible, turn it to the sales team, and track the results for your own records to use at Performance Review time.

Non-Profits: A non-profit is just a business with a cause that doesn't retain profits – well, hopefully they are run like a business. Don't discount non-profits. They need products/services, too. The decision maker is often the executive director, though, and they are almost always in meetings or out at meetings.

Or, it happens too that the executive director must present every decision to a board, making them an information gatherer. A tough go. You sometimes encounter an assistant who books their calendar and can pass information back and forth. Build rapport, make an alliance, be an ally. Remember, you are also an assistant. The assistant can likely give you the road map to succeed with their organization.

Managing Receptionists

In general, follow the phone contact guidelines below for your scheduled follow-ups for a month. Other than your initial call/voicemail to your DM group before you put them back into your general DM group, only Renewals, Scheduled CBs, Prospects, and Appointment Confirmations go in your scheduled follow-up task list. Once you've attempted to reach the decision maker every two to three days for two weeks, space calls to once or twice a week for the last two weeks. If you are not successful in contacting a decision maker by phone after a month of effort, schedule them for a quarterly, bi-annual or annual email marketing campaign according to what seems appropriate for your company's product/service. It may seem appropriate, based on your company's product/service cycle, to also schedule these contacts back into your regular phone rotation on a quarterly, bi-annual or annual basis. Think about when it makes sense to attempt to reach them by phone again.

<u>Screened</u> – if a receptionist screened ("what is this regarding," etc.), make a note. Schedule a call back a <u>week out</u>.

<u>Took Msg</u> – if no DM voicemail, so receptionist had to take a message, make a note. Schedule a call back <u>three days out</u>.

<u>Cranky</u> – if receptionist was "cranky" with your call, make a note. Schedule a call back a <u>week out</u>.

<u>DM not in, in mtg, busy, unavailable</u> – if receptionist said DM is not in or they are in a meeting or they are busy (may say unavailable – clarify as stated above), make a note. Use your discretion considering your schedule. Should you try back later today? If it sounds like you have a good chance of catching the DM, call back today. Otherwise, schedule a call back <u>two days out</u>.

<u>DM not in yet</u> – if receptionist said DM is not in yet, use your discretion considering your schedule. If you think it is worth it, ask receptionist when they are expected, make a note and call them back later today. Realize that unless you ask if this is their regular schedule, it may only be for today. Clarify and make a note. If you now know it is regular, schedule them for a call back the <u>next day</u> within their regular schedule.

<u>DM "in and out"</u> – if receptionist said the DM doesn't have a set schedule, that they are "in and out," make a note and use your discretion. If you don't think it is likely to catch the DM, you may want to make sure you have their email, if possible, send an email, then change their Status ID to "Hold," occasionally sending them marketing emails.

<u>DM works offsite</u> – if the receptionist said the DM works offsite, or at home, or after hours, make a note. You'll never reach them by phone, unless you can get their cell phone or direct

number, which occasionally happens – but, tread lightly here. Make sure you have their email, if possible, send an email, then change their Status ID to "Hold," occasionally sending them marketing emails.

Managing Decision Makers

You have a decision maker's direct extension or cell number. There are guidelines for each step of contact:

Sent intro email – You sent your first email. Schedule call back for two days out.

Sent intro email & left f/u vm - You sent your first email and left a follow-up voicemail on the DM's voicemail. Schedule call back for two days out. Then call every two days for one to two weeks, using your discretion. After two weeks, call once a week, for a month. After a month, unless you have specific information otherwise, schedule a quarterly, bi-annual or annual follow-up. You could set them for a quarterly marketing email campaign, hopefully sending a resource they would find helpful, or a quarterly call. After a month of steady calling, what you do next depends on what intel you have about them. Do you have renewal/review information? If you do, this will guide your scheduling. What is the nature of your company's product/service? Is it seasonal? Are there times of the year that are better to call for your product/service? Factor all of this information in to your decision. You want to "stay in touch" – but as a respectful ally.

Managing Emails

What sort of marketing email campaign you implement has a lot to do with your company, your product/service as well as respecting your decision maker. But I'll state the obvious.

Looking in the Mirror, you know when anyone you do business with is crossing the line from helpful to annoying. Apply that to your own email campaigns.

Product/Service Seasonal, Quarterly, Bi-Annually, Annually is unlikely to offend anyone. I personally feel annoyed receiving emails more often than that, unless it is someone I'm doing a lot of business with, and then I do depend on monthly or even weekly updates. But that is not your situation – you're not yet in that door. Be respectful. You also need to think about what you are sending. Are you sending the same introduction email over and over and over? Switch it up! Add a useful link or tips or resources. Again, look in the Mirror – if you were the decision maker, is there some bit of information you would appreciate?

Managing Voicemail Messages

Why leave messages? Cold-call/blitz advocates would tell you to never leave voicemail messages. They would say that leaving voicemails gives away your power. They would point out that you never get called back, so why leave a message?

We're back to looking in the Mirror. We leave a message because, if we want to be taken serious as being genuinely interested in initiating a professional business relationship, we need to leave an introduction message, preferably after we've sent an introduction email.

Remember, these are two of our at least five positive impressions we need to even gain our contacts' attention. And that is what you would expect from someone courting your business, right?

Think of yourself, and think of a cold caller/blitzer's chances of earning your business compared to a Mirror Marketer who is willing to invest their time in first sending an old-fashioned letter of introduction via email, then calling as promised in the email and leaving a message. Who has a better chance? Who do you see as serious? Who has shown you respect? Who is being transparent and straight with you? We all know the answer to those questions. This is why, as Mirror Marketers, we take the time to send an introduction email and leave an introduction voicemail.

So what do you say? I actually just say a version of my Decision Maker phone script. Something like:

"Hi ___, this is (your name) over at (sales agent's name) office, with (your company name). I'm following up on the email I sent you. (Sales agent's name) asked me to give you a call. We weren't sure (qualifier). (Sales agent's name) was hoping to provide you with a (your product/service) comparison to see if we're a fit, if you were open to that. My direct line is (your phone & direct extension), again that's (repeat phone #), and I'll try to reach you again as well. Thank you. Good-bye."

Any voicemails I would leave after this one would be following up on their request for a call-back, so it would be specific to our last conversation, just like any other follow-up call you would make to anyone else in your life. You're following through on what you said you would do – call them back. So make sure you leave that voicemail, so they know you kept your promise, layering on more positive impressions.

How many voicemails to leave? The only "unsolicited" voicemail I leave is the introduction voicemail, preferably after sending an introduction email. If you are unable to obtain their email from the receptionist, then go ahead and leave an introduction voicemail, making sure to say that last line, *"...I'll try to reach you again,"* leaving the door open for future contact. But while I have them now on a contact schedule for the next month, I really don't leave additional voicemails unless I've reached the decision maker and have gained their permission to follow-up. Why? Because looking in the Mirror, this is what I would want. Wouldn't you? If you don't succeed in reaching them with a regular call schedule of every couple days, then once a week over the course of a month, then let them go for awhile, put them on say a quarterly email campaign, and revisit a regular call schedule say six months from now. The call schedule you determine all depends on the cycle of your product/service.

Remember, as a Mirror Marketer, you realize immediate gratification is a short-sighted illusion and are willing to make the investment necessary to creating those delayed gratification, long-term prospect relationships. As you continue to build your Mirror Appointment Setting pipeline, your rewards begin a sustainable, steady flow.

Call Back Requests

Obviously, if either the receptionist or the decision maker indicates in some way when is a good time to call – even if it is next year -- schedule your call back to honor their request.

These general guidelines are your "rule of thumb," but they cannot replace your knowledge of each situation, your logic and common sense. Always apply your Mirror strategic marketing skills to winning our Ladder game – if that means overriding these guidelines, so be it.

Managing Daily Tasks:

In our *Day in the Life of a Mirror Marketer* screenplay, we took you through your first day. But now, imagine you have mostly weeded out the Discard Status IDs and you have contacts at every step of our Status ID Ladder Game. What does your daily schedule look like? Remember call times always need to be your contacts' time, if you're calling contacts outside your time zone. Here's a priority breakout for you:

> 9-9:30am – Dial "Leads" with qualifier script – majority of decision makers not in yet

> 9:30am – until finished or noon:

  • CRM – Today's Follow-up List – Confirm "Appointments"
    o fill in Daily Contact Report
    o email sales appointments confirmed

  • CRM – Today's Follow-up List – Dial "Prospects"
    o fill in results on Daily Contact Report

  • CRM – Today's Follow-up List – Dial 1st contact "DMs"
    o leave intro email follow-up voicemail if decision maker not reached
    o remove call schedule to return to "DM" group after intro email & voicemail

> Noon – 1pm:

  • Dial "Leads" using qualifier script
    o if decision maker identified, make notes and set Status ID to "DM" to move to DM group
    o if discard, make notes and set to appropriate Status ID to weed out of Leads

> 1pm – 4pm:

  • CRM Today's Follow-up List – Attempt again to confirm "Appointments" not directly reached in the morning
    o fill in Daily Contact Report
    o email sales appointments confirmed

- CRM Today's Follow-up List - Dial any contacts receptionists indicated afternoon best to call
- Email Campaigns
  - o send emails scheduled
  - o fill in Daily Contact Report
- Dial "DM" group using decision maker script
  - o if decision maker reached:
    - Appointment – fill in CRM fields, notes, schedule, Daily Contact Report, set Status ID to "Appointment," send confirmation email to prospect & sales
    - Future Contact – fill in notes, schedule, Daily Contact Report, set Status ID to "Prospect"
    - Hang-up – fill in notes, set Status ID to "Hold"
    - Dead or DNC – fill in notes, set Status ID to "Dead" or "DNC"
- Organize/Email/Dial "Holds" group
- ➤ 4-5pm:
  - Dial "Leads" group using qualifier script – majority of decision makers have left for the day
  - Run Contact Activity Report – Fill in remaining information on Daily Contact Report and submit

Congratulations! Your day is done!

We've completed your training as a Mirror Marketer. There are more nuances, variables and exceptions than I could ever cover here, as you most likely are beginning to realize by now. Just remember, to figure out any new situation – look in the Mirror and LISTEN. That truly is all you need to do to "think in the moment." You were hired because you expressed the ability to do that, so trust it. I hope you find the details and guidelines useful – but "look in the Mirror and LISTEN" really is the most important message I hope you take away. Together, we've built our lean Mirror Appointment Setting machine – take it out for a spin and enjoy the ride.

Conclusion

I was inspired to write this book by unmet potential – by excellent marketers I have come in behind in my troubleshooting whose abilities were clouded by a lack of proper CRM training and a moldy lead list, and by great companies with good intentions to create a successful phone marketing program whose techniques lacked a stable, sustainable foundation.

For call centers and cold call/blitz advocates who may be reading this book, I invite you to board the Mirror Business Strategies train. Please know I've been where you are – both as a telemarketer and manager of telemarketing programs. We're all after results.

I maintain it does matter how we get there, and over 30+ years, I've proven time and again that I can get "how did you do that" results following my Mirror approach that I just can't get without it. It's that simple.

When you really think about it, the Golden Rule, the Mirror, is such a common sense idea – but actually quite revolutionary to put into play. That proof lies in the subtle details I've shared with you here. That proof lies in your intentional decision to shake your paradigm loose from your own WIFM and focus entirely on your prospects WIFM instead, treating them the way you would want to be treated. I challenge you to look in the Mirror and put it into play throughout your business, throughout your life – and prosper!

I now turn to the prequel to this book – Mirror Business. Thank you for your patronage, your time and attention – I appreciate it! I hope I can continue to earn your patronage, time and attention with the entire Mirror Business Strategies series.

Your feedback is important to me:

What do you think of the book? If you liked this book, please take a moment to leave an honest review on Amazon.com. It helps me sell books and I would be very grateful!

Link to Amazon review page: http://bit.ly/uReview

Or…, spread the word by sharing the link to my website with your friends: http://aren-benoit.eliyora.com/

Your friends will thank you almost as much as I do.

…… Aren

About the Author

Aren Benoit's Mirror Business Strategies® were developed over 30+ years as a successful business development specialist in a wide array of industries. Aren has a B.S. in journalism, with a concentration in marketing communications, and PhD studies in social psychology from the University of Colorado-Boulder.

Connect with Aren:

- **Twitter:** https://twitter.com/ArenBenoit
- **LinkedIn:** http://www.linkedin.com/in/arenbenoit
- **Amazon Author Profile:** http://www.amazon.com/Aren-Benoit/e/B00CP6DAFE/
- **Website:** http://aren-benoit.eliyora.com/

Bibliography

Chandler-Pepelnjak, John; Song, Young-Bean. (Retrieved 5/1/13). Optimal Frequency – The Impact of Frequency on Conversion Rates. Atlas Institute. (Charny, E.J. 1966). Psychosomatic manifestations of rapport in psycho-therapy. Psychosomatic Medicine, 28. 305-315. http://atlassolutions.com/wwdocs/user/atlassolutions/en-us/insights/OptFrequency.pdf

Cornell University Ergonomics Web (Retrieved 5-1-13). How to Choose an Ergonomic Chair. http://ergo.human.cornell.edu/AHTutorials/chairch.html.

Herman Miller. (Retrieved 5/1/13). Everybody Deserves a Good Chair. http://www.hermanmiller.com/content/hermanmiller/english/research/research-summaries/everybody-deserves-a-good-chair.html

Herman Miller. (Retrieved 5/1/13). If The Chair Fits. http://www.hermanmiller.com/content/hermanmiller/english/research/research-summaries/if-the-chair-fits.html.

Herman Miller. (Retrieved 5/1/13). New Directions in Call Center Design. http://www.hermanmiller.com/content/dam/hermanmiller/documents/research_summaries/wp_Call_Center_Design.pdf

Iacoboni, Marco (2009). Imitation, Empathy and Mirror Neurons. Annual Review of Psychology, 60:653-70.

Kendon, A. (1970). Movement coordination in social interactiorl. Acta Psychologica, 32, 100-125.

127

LaFrance, M. (1979). Nonverbal synchrony and rapport: Analysis by the cross-lag panel technique. Social Psychology Quarterly, 42. 66-70.

LaFrance, M. (1985). Postural mirroring and intergroup relations. Personality and Social Psychology Bulletin, 11, 207

MecLabs Marketing Sherpa. (Retrieved 5/1/13). New Online Study Data: Clicks and Conversions Plummet After Five Impressions. http://www.marketingsherpa.com/article/clicks-conversions-plummet-after-five#

Nasa Spinoff. (Retrieved 5/1/13). Ergonomic Chairs.http://spinoff.nasa.gov/spinoff1997/ch2.html

Scheflen, A. E. (1964). The significance of posture in communication systems. Psychiatp, 27. 316-331.

Singh, Nisheeth. (Retrieved 5/1/13). How Many Times Should You Call Each Sales Lead. Lead Critic: http://www.coffeeforclosers.org/how-many-times-should-you-call-each-sales-lead-read-our-new-call-attempts-study/.

Tickle-Degnen, Linda; Rosenthal, Robert (1990). "The nature of rapport and its nonverbal correlates". Psychological Inquiry 1: 285–293.

Wikipedia. (Retrieved 5/1/13). Effective Frequency. http://en.wikipedia.org/wiki/Effective_frequency.

Wikipedia. (Retrieved 5/1/13) Handshake. http://en.wikipedia.org/wiki/Handshake#cite_note-3.

~~**~~

Made in the USA
Las Vegas, NV
18 March 2022